Michael Gienger

HEALING CRYSTALS

The A-Z Guide to 430 Gemstones

Translated from the German
by Chinwendu Uzodike

D0048558

EARTHDANCER

A FINDHORN PRESS IMPRINT

Publisher's note
The information in this volume has been compiled according to the best of our knowledge and belief, and the healing properties of the crystals have been tested many times over. Bearing in mind that different people react in different ways, neither the publisher nor the author can give a guarantee for the effectiveness or safety of use in individual cases. In the case of serious health problems please consult your doctor or naturopath.

1 2 3 4 5 6 7 8 9 10 11 12 13 12 11 10 09 08 07 06 05

Healing Crystals – Michael Gienger
With photos by Ines Blersch

Published by Earthdancer Books, an Imprint of :
Findhorn Press, 305a The Park, Forres IV36 3TE, Scottland.
www.earthdancer.co.uk   ·   www.findhornpress.com

This English edition © 2005 Earthdancer Books
English translation © 2005 Chinwendu Uzodike
Editing of the translated text by Roselle Angwin

Originally published in German as *Heilsteine, 430 Steine von A-Z*

World copyright © 2003 Neue Erde GmbH, Saarbruecken, Germany
Original German text copyright © 2003 Michael Gienger

Cover photography: Ines Blersch
Cover and book design: Dragon Design UK
Typeset in News Gothic
Printed and bound by Legoprint S.p.A., Italy.

ISBN 1-84409-067-1

A simple guide to using gemstones

Twenty years after the first wave of modern publications on the healing power of gemstones, Michael Gienger now presents a simple illustrated guide to currently existing healing gemstones. As a pioneer and one of the most committed researchers in the field of gem remedies, he has succeeded in portraying the specific healing properties of 430 crystals in a simple and compact form, whilst still giving a precise description of each crystal and clearly differentiating between them.

This work reflects the development in the field of gem remedies over three spans of seven years: seven years of pioneering work, seven years of systematic research and seven years of working experience – without these preliminary stages and the co-operation of many naturopaths, doctors and gemstone consultants, this work would not have been possible. My heartfelt thanks go to all those who have contributed to making this work a reality!

This guide is intended for all those who seek a reliable and simple source of information on healing crystals:

- For all interested people who wish to inform themselves about the healing properties of crystals.

- For all naturopaths, doctors and gemstone consultants as an up-to-date reference guide to healing crystals.

- For all those who work with or deal in crystals, as an important update on the latest developments in the field of gem remedies.

In a word: a guide for anyone who relates to crystals. So take a look ...

How to use this guide

This guide presents and defines the mineralogy and healing effects of crystals in common use. It offers brief information on the basic properties of the crystals. For further information, consult the indicated bibliography as needed. Terms used in the guide are explained in detail as follows:

Title: the title of each entry gives the name or names of the illustrated crystal. In addition to mineralogical names, their common names are also used if they better pinpoint or describe the crystal in question. To distinguish the mineralogical names, which are scientifically recognised, from the common, or trade, names, they are printed in black, while the common names are printed in **blue**. In certain cases the blue names are chosen titles which serve as a suggestion, to both gemstone dealers and interested readers, of correct and clear designation of the crystals, including their healing properties.

Mineralogy: this gives brief information on the mineralogy, especially the crystal classification and group where necessary, as well as the crystalline structure and nature of formation ('primary' = molten magma formation, 'secondary' = formation through disintegration and deposits, 'tertiary' = metamorphic formation under heat and pressure). In addition to the visible colour, these details are very important for the healing effect and usage of a crystal. Their significance can be found in Michael Gienger's book *Crystal Power, Crystal Healing* (Cassell London 1998).

Indications: this gives information on the important healing effects and areas of activity of respective crystals. It particularly presents those major properties that characterise the crystal in question and distinguish it from crystals with similar properties. Other healing effects can be looked up in the indicated bibliography.

(**SP**) refers to the 'spirit or spiritual aspect', the innate nature of a person including his or her important intentions, aims and focus in life; (**S**) refers to the 'soul or the subconscious', including temperament, emotions, intuitive perceptions, dreams, psychological experiences, habits and unconscious reactions; (**M**) refers to 'mind or mental aspects', including ideas, values, convictions, views as well as the manner of thinking and conscious action; (**B**) refers to the 'body or physical aspect', the human organism as a whole with its senses, organs and functions.

Defining these four aspects clearly differentiates what can be influenced, enhanced, changed or cured with the help of the crystals.

Bib.: this information refers to comprehensive literature in which the crystal in question, or at least crystals of the same kind or family, are described. The numbers 1 to 4 refer to the bibliography on page 95.

Rarity: this gives an estimate of the availability of the crystal in question. Naturally this is often prone to a lot of variation depending on which crystals are collected or mined in which mines or discovery sites at each point in time. As a result these estimates are never 'absolute'! They are only intended to give a clue as to the chances of finding a desired crystal in the shops in the foreseeable future. Also the availability of a crystal does not always have to do with how rare or common it is. Rare crystals that are well known are sometimes more available than more common but less known ones. The availability has been individually classified as follows:

Common: means it has been continuously available in large quantities over a long period of time and cut into different forms and shapes. No scarcity of the common shapes or forms is anticipated in the foreseeable future.

Readily available: means sufficiently available most times. No major scarcities of particular forms are expected in the future.

Not always available: means not always obtainable. Sometimes there is a scarcity or just a few forms are available in limited quantities. The reserves are unsteady or limited.

Scarce: means hardly available. There is a frequent scarcity over long periods of time. It is sometimes only available in very few forms. Reserves are very limited.

Rare: means extremely scarce and obtainable only at definite times. For such crystals there is only a minimal reserve, or the known discovery sites are already completely exhausted or no longer accessible.

○ This little tick box enables you to make a note of the crystals you have – giving you an overview of crystals in your collection, first aid kit, experiment kit or therapy repertoire.

Abalone (Paua shell, Mother-of-pearl)
Mineralogy: coloured shell (Aragonite, orthorhombic, secondary)
Indications: (SP) cheerfulness, security, protection (S) helps overcome despondency, insecurity and disappointment (M) ensures careful dealing with oneself and others (B) ameliorates irritation and inflammations of skin, mucous membrane and sensory organs.
Bib.: [2]   **Rarity:** common ○

Actinolite
Mineralogy: chain silicate of the Amphibole group (monocl., tert.)
Indications: (SP) straightforwardness, new orientation, determination (S) promotes self-esteem and inner balance (M) helps pursue personal aims appropriately (B) stimulates activities of the liver and kidney as well as all building-up and growth processes.
Bib.: [1] [2]   **Rarity:** not always available ○

Actinolite with Chlorite
Mineralogy: chain silicate rich in minerals (monoclinic, tertiary)
Indications: (SP) success through calm tenacity (S) brings patience, perseverance and self-confidence (M) makes decision-making easier (B) stimulates activities of the liver and kidneys as well as all fortifying and growth processes of the body.
Bib.: [1] [2]   **Rarity:** not always available ○

Actinolite Quartz
Mineralogy: actinolite in quartz crystal (monoclinic/trigonal, primary)
Indications: (SP) new orientation, awareness, course correction (S) enhances sense of right timing (M) aids in overcoming weaknesses and mistakes (B) stimulates the liver and kidneys as well as metabolism; detoxification and excretion.
Bib.: [1] [2]   **Rarity:** scarce ○

Aegirine
Mineralogy: chain silicate of the pyroxene group (monocl., prim.)
Indications: (SP) sincerity, virtue (S) promotes self-respect, helpful with relationship problems, separation or grief (M) focusing on major goals (B) good for backaches and pains, for nerves, muscles, bones and hormonal glands.
Bib.: [4]   **Rarity:** scarce ○

Aegirine-Augite
Mineralogy: chain silicate of the pyroxene group (monocl., prim.)
Indications: (SP) posture; perseverance (S) encourages patience, helps maintain composure in difficult situations (M) for work requiring patience (B) enhances digestion, activities of the intestine, kidneys as well as that of the hormonal glands; ameliorates pain.
Bib.: –   **Rarity:** scarce ○

Agate
Mineralogy: banded quartz (silicon dioxide, trigonal, primary)
Indications: (SP) inner stability, composure, maturity (S) protection, warmth, security, self-confidence (M) sense of reality, pragmatic thinking (B) for the eyes, hollow organs (like the stomach, intestines etc.), blood vessels and skin. Protective stone during pregnancy.
Bib.: [1] [2] [3]   **Rarity:** common ○

Agate (with cell-like markings)
Mineralogy: agate with cell/tissue type signs (trigonal, primary)
Indications: (SP) versatility, regeneration (S) revives dazed frame of mind (M) enhances concentration on the essential (B) for tissues, metabolism, immune system; good for infections and skin diseases.
Bib.: [2] [3]   **Rarity:** not always available ○

Agate (Dendritic Agate)
Mineralogy: agate with fern-like manganese markings (trig., prim.)
Indications: (SP) integrity, purification (S) helps overcome emotional boundary violations and emotional strain (M) lends ability to examine and resolve unpleasant issues (B) for tissue detoxification in problems of the skin, mucous membrane, lungs and intestine.
Bib.: [1] [2] [3]   **Rarity:** not always available ○

Agate (Eye Agate)
Mineralogy: agate with eye-shaped markings (trigonal, primary)
Indications: (SP) interest, resistance, protection (S) perseverance, also in the face of nightmares (M) helps face facts (B) for inflammation of the eyes, problems of the conjunctiva or retina, glaucoma, blood vessels and prostate.
Bib.: [1] [2] [3]   **Rarity:** readily available ○

Agate (Fire Agate)
Mineralogy: agate with iridescent iron oxides (trigonal, primary)
Indications: (SP) initiative, commitment (S) cheerfulness, contentment (M) vigour, positive thinking, understanding experiences (B) for excretion, problems of the intestine, especially flatulence, diarrhoea, constipation, (chronic) inflammation.
Bib.: [2] [3]   Rarity: scarce ○

Agate (Fortification Agate with bladder-like markings)
Mineralogy: agate with bladder-like markings (trigonal, primary)
Indications: (SP) self control, letting go, inner calm (S) setting bounds, relaxation (M) helps to resolutely implement one's ideas or projects (B) for bladder problems, especially infections, urinary retention, incontinence and prostate.
Bib.: [1] [2] [3]   Rarity: readily available ○

Agate (with inflammation markings)
Mineralogy: agate with natural pink colour (trigonal, primary)
Indications: (SP) transformation, consolation, appeasement (S) renewed confidence in unpleasant situations (M) careful mastering of difficulties (B) for inflammation of all organs or tissues; enhances perspiration during fever.
Bib.: [1] [2] [3]   Rarity: not always available ○

Agate (Lace Agate, Crazy Lace)
Mineralogy: agate with twisting & turning bands (trigonal, primary)
Indications: (SP) elegance, mental agility, dynamism (S) liveliness, variety (M) flexibility in thinking and acting (B) promotes tissue metabolism, very effective against infections, insect bites, varicose veins and haemorrhoids.
Bib.: [2] [3]   Rarity: readily available ○

Agate (Layered Agate, Banded Agate)
Mineralogy: agate with band-like layers (trigonal, primary)
Indications: (SP) steadfastness and unity (S) protection, security, moral stability (M) for pragmatic planning in thinking and actions (B) for the intestine and digestion; improves elasticity of blood vessel walls and prevents varicose veins.
Bib.: [1] [2] [3]   Rarity: readily available ○

Agate, pink (Apricot Agate)

Mineralogy: agate, predominantly pink coloured (trigonal, primary)
Indications: (SP) incentive, compassion (S) steadfastness, protection and safety (M) helps to actively deal with difficult assignments (B) for inflammation; activates absorption of nutrients in the intestine and also stimulates metabolism and blood circulation.
Bib.: [2] [3] Rarity: not always available ○

Agate, red (Blood Agate)

Mineralogy: agate with a natural red colour (trigonal, primary)
Indications: (SP) strength, stability, increases stamina (S) perseverance and strength generated from inner balance (M) development and conscious usage of personal abilities (B) fortifies stomach, intestine and blood vessels, enhances circulation and blood-flow.
Bib.: [1] [2] Rarity: readily available ○

Agate (with scar images)

Mineralogy: agate with scar-like images (trigonal, primary)
Indications: (SP) amendment, eases burdens (S) overcome past injuries (M) helps to actively cope with stress and strain (B) improves skin and tissue metabolism, enhances wound healing, and reduces scar formation.
Bib.: [2] [3] Rarity: not always available ○

Agate (with skin-like image)

Mineralogy: agate, similar to layers of the skin (trigonal, primary)
Indications: (SP) contact, setting bounds (S) stability and perseverance (M) constructive reflection (B) regulates, builds up, detoxifies the skin, for rashes, inflammations, fungal infections, as well as dry, chapped or impure skin.
Bib.: [1] [2] [3] Rarity: readily available ○

Agate (Snakeskin Agate)

Mineralogy: agate, similar to the skin of a snake (trigonal, primary)
Indications: (SP) clarification, communication (S) calms agitated emotions (M) for realistic thinking and well-considered actions (B) good for the brain, metabolism, lymph and body fluids, decongests mucous and ameliorates allergies.
Bib.: [2] Rarity: scarce ○

Agate (Star Agate, Thunderegg, Amulet stone)
Mineralogy: agate in a rhyolite or porphyrite nodule (trig., prim.)
Indications: (SP) consciousness, alertness, maturity (S) good perceptive faculty in a state of inner stability; reduces stress (M) for good understanding and promotes inference skills (B) for the brain, spinal cord, nerves, liver, immune system and hormone balance.
Bib.: [2]   **Rarity:** not always available ○

Agate (with stomach-like markings)
Mineralogy: agate with stomach like markings (trigonal, primary)
Indications: (SP) life experience, work (S) enhances absorption of impressions and experiences (M) promotes learning and sober reflection (B) for digestion and metabolism, for stomach and intestine problems e.g. nausea or gastritis.
Bib.: [1] [2] [3]   **Rarity:** readily available ○

Agate (Tubular Agate)
Mineralogy: agate with tube-like inclusions (trigonal, primary)
Indications: (SP) unfolding, progress (S) tenacity, acceptance of the inevitable (M) insight, reconsider views (B) promotes activity of the glands and metabolism; very effective for prostate, bladder and digestive problems; aids sexual endeavours.
Bib.: [2]   **Rarity:** readily available ○

Agate (with uterus-shaped markings)
Mineralogy: agate, with uterus-shaped markings (trigonal, primary)
Indications: (SP) growth, development, blossom (S) instils deep security when homesick or lonely (M) cautiousness (B) for inflammation of the uterus, menstrual pain, pregnancy and normalisation after childbirth.
Bib.: [1] [2] [3]   **Rarity:** readily available ○

Agate (Water Agate, Enhydro)
Mineralogy: agate nodule filled with water (trigonal, primary)
Indications: (SP) growth, protection, development (S) instils deep security and enhances inner peace, promotes empathy (M) fortifies solicitude and openness (B) protective stone in pregnancy; regulates water and hormone balance.
Bib.: [1] [2] [3]   **Rarity:** scarce ○

Agate, white (Peace Agate)

Mineralogy: colourless, white agate (trigonal, primary)
Indications: (SP) calm, peace, self-confidence (S), strengthens inner composure, for kindness, sincerity and light-heartedness (M) promotes tolerance and understanding (B) for the eyes, brain, skin, lymph and tissues; protective stone in pregnancy.
Bib.: [2]   **Rarity:** readily available ○

Agate, white/black (Zebra Agate)

Mineralogy: agate with black/white stripes (trigonal, primary)
Indications: (SP) reformation, reflection, maturity (S) promotes objectivity and straightforwardness (M) enhances meticulousness; for objective and rational ordering of one's life (B) improves activities of motor nerves, sense of hearing and balance.
Bib.: [2]   **Rarity:** not always available ○

Agatised Coral (Petoskey Stone)

Mineralogy: fossilised corals (quartz, trigonal, secondary)
Indications: (SP) self-expression; hospitality (S) eases fear as well as emotional and social strain (M) promotes ability to communicate, team spirit and synergy in partnership (B) helps with breathing difficulties, cramped bronchial tubes and cough.
Bib.: [2]   **Rarity:** scarce ○

Alabaster (Gypsum)

Mineralogy: fine crystalline calcium sulphate (monocl., second.)
Indications: (SP) stability, self-control, setting bounds (S) helps set boundaries and stabilise labile psychic state, protects in cases of hypersensitivity (M) conscious recognition of old patterns (B) firms up tissues, loosens up hardened muscles (for short-term use only).
Bib.: [2]   **Rarity:** readily available ○

Alabaster Engelberg (Gypsum)

Mineralogy: alabaster nodule from Leonberg (monocl., second)
Indications: (SP) self-awareness, setting bounds (S) for calm and relaxation, helps overcome old habits, intensifies dreams (M) helps place priorities (B) for restful sleep, improves well-being, alleviates pain and releases tension.
Bib.: [2]   **Rarity:** scarce ○

11

Albite (Feldspar)

Mineralogy: sodium feldspar (lattice silicate, triclinic, primary)
Indications: **(SP)** intuitive perception, broadens horizons **(S)** brings relief, opening and broad vision **(M)** improves perceptive faculty, helps recognise new perspectives in life **(B)** for flexible muscles, pliable tissues and healthy skin.
Bib.: [2]   **Rarity:** not always available ○

Alexandrite

Mineralogy: colour changing chrysoberyl (orthorhombic, tertiary)
Indications: **(SP)** inspiration and willpower **(S)** intensifies dreams and perception of emotions **(M)** promotes power of imagination, willingness to take risks and perception of inner voice **(B)** for disorders of the nerves and senses; helps with inflammations, stimulates the liver.
Bib.: [1] [2]   **Rarity:** rare ○

Alunite (Alumstone)

Mineralogy: alkaline potassium aluminium sulphate (trig., tert.)
Indications: **(SP)** comfort, modesty **(S)** settles discords, disperses fear and guilty conscience **(M)** encourages frugality and being reserved **(B)** helps in cases of inflammations, eczema and rashes as well as radiation damage.
Bib.: [2]   **Rarity:** not always available ○

Amazonite (Feldspar)

Mineralogy: potassium feldspar (lattice silicate, triclinic, prim./tert.)
Indications: **(SP)** self-determination **(S)** emotional balance **(M)** harmonious interaction of intellect and intuition **(B)** regulates metabolic disorders (liver); harmonises the brain, vegetative nervous system, internal organs; facilitates childbirth.
Bib.: [1] [2]   **Rarity:** readily available ○

Amber

Mineralogy: fossiliferous resin (organic, amorphous, secondary)
Indications: **(SP)** makes carefree **(S)** for cheerfulness and trust **(M)** strengthens belief in oneself **(B)** good for the stomach, spleen, gallbladder, liver, joints, skin, mucous membranes, glands and intestine; aids teething in children; helps with allergies, rheumatism and diabetes.
Bib.: [1] [2] [3]   **Rarity:** common ○

Amethyst, banded (Chevron Amethyst)

Mineralogy: violet/white striped crystal quartz (trigonal, primary)
Indications: (SP) sobriety, purity, composure, calm **(S)** peps up in cases of perpetual tiredness, resolves persistent anxiety **(M)** helps overcome habitual tendencies and addictions **(B)** good for the lungs, large intestine and skin; alleviates itching and sunburn.
Bib.: [1] [2] [3]   **Rarity:** common ○

Amethyst with Chalcedony

Mineralogy: amethyst with chalcedony stripes (trigonal, primary)
Indications: (SP) reconciliation, peace, kindness **(S)** promotes feelings of happiness and universal love **(M)** helps with self-reconciliation and reconciliation among people **(B)** cleanses the body fluids and harmonises the whole organism.
Bib.: [1]   **Rarity:** scarce ○

Amethyst, dark purple

Mineralogy: very deep violet crystal quartz (trigonal, primary)
Indications: (SP) uprightness, impartiality **(S)** willpower, helps overcome pain, grief and losses **(M)** improves concentration, helps ward off external influences **(B)** alleviates pain, bruises and swellings; good for diarrhoea.
Bib.: [1] [2] [3]   **Rarity:** scarce ○

Amethyst, light purple (Cape Amethyst)

Mineralogy: light violet crystal quartz (trigonal, primary)
Indications: (SP) peace, spirituality, clarification, meditation **(S)** for intuition, good clear dreams, improves fitful sleep **(M)** enhances conscious perception and understanding experiences **(B)** good for headaches, the lungs, skin and nerves.
Bib.: [1] [2] [3]   **Rarity:** common ○

Amethyst, medium purple

Mineralogy: dark violet crystal quartz (trigonal, primary)
Indications: (SP) alertness, justice, inner peace **(S)** helps overcome grief and losses **(M)** awareness, sense of judgement, constructive thinking and acting **(B)** good for the skin; alleviates pain, tension and lowers high blood pressure.
Bib.: [1] [2] [3]   **Rarity:** readily available ○

Ametrine
Mineralogy: yellow/violet crystal quartz (trigonal, primary)
Indications: (SP) cheerful composure, a fulfilled existence (S) optimism, joie de vivre, feeling of well-being (M) helps retain creativity and dynamism in the face of all challenges (B) balances out body tension, harmonises the vegetative nervous system and body metabolism.
Bib.: [1] [2]   Rarity: scarce ○

Ammolite (Korite, Calcentine)
Mineralogy: ammonite shell made of Aragonite (orthorh., second.)
Indications: (SP) harmony, dignity, splendour (S) for sense of beauty, seductive charm, charisma (M) awakens interest in mysteries, releases mental obsessions (B) normalises cell metabolism, energy output, heartbeat and fortifies the heart.
Bib.: –   Rarity: rare ○

Andalusite
Mineralogy: aluminium island silicate (orthorh., prim./tert.)
Indications: (SP) self-recognition, discovery of personal vocation (S) promotes self-confidence and generosity (M) helps to think big and be realistic at the same time (B) enhances de-acidification, good for stomach and intestine problems; has a strengthening effect.
Bib.: [2]   Rarity: not always available ○

Anhydrite (Angelite)
Mineralogy: anhydrous calcium sulphate (orthorhombic, secondary)
Indications: (SP) stability, stamina (S) helps withstand extreme psychic strain and overcome insecurity (M) ends fruitless brooding and helps give up obsessions (B) stimulates the kidney function, water balance and reduction of oedema.
Bib.: [2]   Rarity: not always available ○

Anthophyllite
Mineralogy: anthophyllite/staurolite rock (orthorhombic, tertiary)
Indications: (SP) self-esteem, acknowledgement (S) releases stress and self-created pressure (M) helps create and maintain room for personal interest (B) helps with nervous diseases as well as with problems of the kidneys and ears.
Bib.: [2] (see Hermanov Balls)   Rarity: scarce ○

Antimonite

Mineralogy: dark grey antimonite sulphide (orthorhombic, primary)
Indications: (SP) harmonises personal interests with higher ideals
(S) helps give up negative habits (M) helps overcome limiting views
(B) helps with problems of the digestive tract (stomach), gum and
skin (peeling).
Bib.: [1] [2] [3]   **Rarity:** not always available ○

Apatite, blue

Mineralogy: blue calcium phosphate (hexagonal, mostly tertiary)
Indications: (SP) motivation (S) stabilises, helps combat listlessness
after over-exertion (M) promotes independence and ambitiousness
(B) builds up, de-acidifies and helps with rickets, arthrosis, osteoporo-
sis and the healing of fractures.
Bib.: [1] [2] [3]   **Rarity:** not always available ○

Apatite, green

Mineralogy: green calcium phosphate (hexagonal, primary/tertiary)
Indications: (SP) sociable (S) livens up, helps combat listlessness
after over-exertion (M) helps live life full of variety (B) builds up, de-
acidifies, enhances formation of cartilage, bones and dentition, also
helps with fractures.
Bib.: [1] [2] [3]   **Rarity:** not always available ○

Apatite, yellow

Mineralogy: yellow calcium phosphate (hexagonal, mostly primary)
Indications: (SP) drive (S) makes extravert, invigorates and livens
up, helps out of state of apathy (M) makes optimistic and hopeful (B)
gives appetite; mobilises energy reserves; improves posture; helps
with problems of the bones, cartilage and joints.
Bib.: [1] [2] [3]   **Rarity:** scarce ○

Aplite (Dalmatian Stone)

Mineralogy: feldspar, quartz, pyroxene (tricl./trig./monocl., prim.)
Indications: (SP) reflection (S) has a fortifying, restorative and emotionally harmonising effect (M) prompts one to carefully think over
plans, reflect on every phase of development and then to carry plans
out with vigour (B) stimulates the nerves and reflex actions.
Bib.: [1] [2]   **Rarity:** readily available ○

Apophyllite, green
Mineralogy: water-containing sheet silicate (tetragonal, primary)
Indications: (SP) liberation, sincerity (S) helps with fear, pressure and feeling of oppression, releases withheld emotions (M) offers a moment of respite after great exertion (B) helps with problems of the nerves, skin and respiratory tract, allergies and asthma.
Bib.: [1] [2] [3]   Rarity: scarce ○

Apophyllite, white
Mineralogy: water-containing sheet silicate (tetragonal, primary)
Indications: (SP) openness, frankness (S) helps overcome insecurity and openly show real nature (M) helps give up anxious tendencies and thought patterns (B) helps with problems of the skin, mucous membrane and respiratory tract, allergies and asthma.
Bib.: [1] [2] [3]   Rarity: readily available ○

Aquamarine
Mineralogy: iron-containing beryl, blue to green (hexag., primary)
Indications: (SP) farsightedness, foresight (S) bestows perseverance, discipline, light heartedness (M) clears up confusion, helps to bring unfinished business to a conclusion (B) helps with allergies, hay fever, problems of the eyes, respiratory tract, thyroid gland and bladder.
Bib.: [1] [2] [3]   Rarity: readily available ○

Aragonite, white
Mineralogy: white calcium carbonate (orthorhombic, secondary)
Indications: (SP) stable development (S) combats oversensitivity, stabilises exceedingly fast developments (M) promotes concentration, calms erratic behaviour (B) improves nervous spasms, strengthens muscles, bones, discs, immune system and improves digestion.
Bib.: [1] [2] [3]   Rarity: not always available ○

Aragonite-Calcite, banded
Mineralogy: calcium carbonate (orthorhombic/trigonal, secondary)
Indications: (SP) promotes growth, unburdens (S) helps live up to expectations, has a calming and motivating effect (M) helps remain focused under intensive strain (B) helps with problems of the stomach, intestine, discs, joints and meniscus.
Bib.: [2]   Rarity: readily available ○

Astrophyllite
Mineralogy: alkaline group silicate (triclinic, primary)
Indications: (SP) inspiration, perceptive faculty (S) receptive to needs, lively dreams (M) helps catch up on unfinished projects, openness, expressive ability (B) for the large intestine and hormone system, very helpful with menstrual and menopausal problems.
Bib.: [2]   **Rarity:** not always available ○

Augite
Mineralogy: chain silicate of the pyroxene group (monocl., primary)
Indications: (SP) composure, stability (S) relieves pressure and strain, gives self-assurance (M) supports active defence against oppressive influences (B) good for problems of the digestive system and the back, especially those caused by emotional strain.
Bib.: [2]   **Rarity:** not always available ○

Aventurine, blue (Blue Quartz Group)
Mineralogy: blue glittering quartz (trigonal, primary)
Indications: (SP) imperturbability (S) calms, relaxes, relieves nervousness (M) helps approach interesting or important projects calmly (B) ameliorates pain and chronic stiffness; has a cooling effect and reduces fever.
Bib.: [2]   **Rarity:** readily available ○

Aventurine, green (Quartz)
Mineralogy: glittering quartz containing fuchsite (trigonal, primary)
Indications: (SP) easy-goingness (S) helps with nervousness, stress and sleep disorders (M) helps free from anxiety and roving thoughts (B) protects against heart attack and arteriosclerosis; alleviates rashes, inflammations, sunburn and sunstroke.
Bib.: [1] [2] [3]   **Rarity:** common ○

Aventurine, orange (Quartz)
Mineralogy: glittering quartz containing hematite (trigonal, primary)
Indications: (SP) cheerfulness (S) promotes a cheerful and relaxed atmosphere (M) enables living one's dreams, promotes a relaxed alertness (B) promotes blood formation, good blood circulation, warms up and revitalises numb parts of the body, fortifies the liver.
Bib.: [2]   **Rarity:** not always available ○

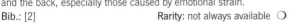

Aventurine, red (Raspberry Quartz)
Mineralogy: glittering quartz containing iron (trig., mostly primary)
Indications: (SP) level-headedness (S) conveys strength and self-assurance (M) helps pursue personal goals in a pragmatic manner (B) stimulates blood circulation, enhances blood flow, nerves and perceptive abilities of the senses and aids sexual endeavours.
Bib.: [2]   **Rarity:** not always available ◯

Azurite
Mineralogy: alkaline copper carbonate (monoclinic, secondary)
Indications: (SP) recognition, experience (S) reveals and helps give up adopted unexamined ideas (M) makes reflective, critical, enhances awareness and self-recognition (B) stimulates the liver, brain, nerves and thyroid gland; improves reflex actions.
Bib.: [1] [2]   **Rarity:** readily available ◯

Azurite-malachite
Mineralogy: alkaline copper carbonate (monoclinic, secondary)
Indications: (SP) harmony, interest (S) makes open-minded, helpful and disperses inner turmoil (M) harmonises the intellect and feelings, helps resolve conflicts (B) normalises disharmonious cell growth, releases cramps, fortifies the liver and detoxifies.
Bib.: [1] [2]   **Rarity:** scarce ◯

Azurite on Pseudomalachite
Mineralogy: copper carbonate/phosphate (monoclinic, secondary)
Indications: (SP) self-confidence (S) helps with tension, nervousness, vulnerability as well as fear of recurring symptoms (M) helps alter paralysing thoughts (B) has a cramp-releasing effect; helps with asthma, stomach problems and disorders of the nerves.
Bib.: –   **Rarity:** rare ◯

Barite (Heavy Spar)
Mineralogy: barium sulphate (orthorhombic, primary or secondary)
Indications: (SP) setting boundaries, importance (S) clears confusion, helps with shyness and anxiety (M) strengthens memory, helps formulate thoughts and words (B) improves posture; good for sore throat and stomachache as well as strong sensitivity to cold.
Bib.: [2]   **Rarity:** not always available ◯

Beryl, colourless (Goshenite)
Mineralogy: beryllium aluminium ring silicate (hexagonal, primary)
Indications: (SP) goal-oriented, efficient **(S)** promotes patience, perseverance, discipline and open-heartedness **(M)** aids intensive learning, care and systematic approach **(B)** helps with short- and long-sightedness; strengthens the nerves, relieves nausea and pain.
Bib.: [1] [2]   **Rarity:** rare ○

Beryl, red (Bixbite)
Mineralogy: beryl containing manganese and lithium (hex., prim.)
Indications: (SP) energises and makes dynamic **(S)** helps with lack of drive, over-exertion and disharmony **(M)** lends vigour to tackle long-postponed unpleasant or difficult issues **(B)** fortifies circulatory system and nerves; helps with aftermath of permanent stress.
Bib.: [1] [2]   **Rarity:** rare ○

Beryl (Vanadium Beryl)
Mineralogy: beryl containing vanadium (hexagonal, primary)
Indications: (SP) care, trust **(S)** helps with lack of courage and despair **(M)** motivates to tackle the seemingly impossible **(B)** fortifies the liver and functional tissue of the organs (parenchyma); detoxifies; helps with inflammations and degeneration processes.
Bib.: [2]   **Rarity:** scarce ○

Biotite Lenses (Birthing Stones)
Mineralogy: magnesium iron mica (monoclinic, tertiary)
Indications: (SP) aids self-realisation **(S)** protects from external influences **(M)** helps with decision-making **(B)** good for hyperacidity, rheumatism, gout, constipation, sciatica and kidney problems; aids childbirth (triggers labour, relaxes the pelvis and softens the neck of the womb).
Bib.: [1] [2] [3]   **Rarity:** rare ○

Brasilianite
Mineralogy: anhydrous, alkaline phosphate (monoclinic, primary)
Indications: (SP) guidance through the higher self **(S)** helps with nightmares, fear and insomnia **(M)** aids viewing things from a higher standpoint **(B)** ameliorates recurring pain, including menstrual pain.
Bib.: [2]   **Rarity:** scarce ○

Bronzite
Mineralogy: chain silicate of the pyroxene group (orthorh., prim.)
Indications: (SP) for inner composure **(S)** lends vigour and inner calm simultaneously, as well as regeneration from chronic exhaustion **(M)** helps retain a clear head and control under permanent stress **(B)** fortifies the nerves, releases cramps and relieves pain.
Bib.: [2] [3]   **Rarity:** readily available ○

Bustamite
Mineralogy: wollastonite containing manganese (triclinic, tertiary)
Indications: (SP) deepens connection with the earth, inner composure **(S)** promotes ability to relax, lends positive disposition to physical nature **(M)** helps focus thoughts and turn them into deeds **(B)** enhances motor nerves as well as sensation in legs and feet.
Bib.: [2]   **Rarity:** scarce ○

Calcite, blue
Mineralogy: blue calcium carbonate (trigonal, secondary)
Indications: (SP) sense of judgement **(S)** calms, makes inwardly stable and confident in appearance **(M)** improves memory and powers of discernment **(B)** good for the lymph, mucous membranes, skin, large intestine, connective tissues, bones and teeth.
Bib.: [1] [2] [3]   **Rarity:** readily available ○

Calcite, clear
Mineralogy: calcium carbonate (trigonal, secondary)
Indications: (SP) for development **(S)** promotes spiritual progress **(M)** makes confident and faster in thinking and acting **(B)** stimulates metabolism; promotes growth in children; fortifies mucous membranes, skin, intestine, connective tissues, bones and teeth.
Bib.: [1] [2] [3]   **Rarity:** common ○

Calcite, green
Mineralogy: green calcium carbonate (trigonal, secondary)
Indications: (SP) makes imaginative **(S)** aids letting go of constraining emotions **(M)** makes more open and interested, helps transform ideas into action **(B)** alleviates inflammation; enhances detoxification; helps with problems of the liver and gallbladder.
Bib.: [1] [2] [3]   **Rarity:** common ○

Calcite, honey-coloured (Honey Calcite)
Mineralogy: iron-containing calcium carbonate (trigonal, secondary)
Indications: (SP) assurance **(S)** promotes a confident and optimistic approach to life **(M)** initiates relying more on one's feeling and sensing **(B)** stimulates digestion, metabolism and excretion; strengthens the intestine, connective tissues, bones and teeth.
Bib.: [1] [2] [3]   **Rarity:** readily available ○

Calcite, orange (Orange Calcite)
Mineralogy: iron-containing calcium carbonate (trigonal, secondary)
Indications: (SP) self-confidence **(S)** promotes self-respect and confidence in one's abilities **(M)** promotes optimism, without becoming unrealistic **(B)** enhances digestion and healing of the connective tissues, skin and bones.
Bib.: [1] [2] [3]   **Rarity:** common ○

Calcite, pink (Mangano Calcite)
Mineralogy: manganese-containing calcium carbonate (trig., sec.)
Indications: (SP) friendliness **(S)** promotes warmth, acceptance, helpfulness, friendly disposition **(M)** makes open-minded and accommodating of others **(B)** strengthens the heart, normalises heartbeat; good for connective tissues, blood vessels and skin.
Bib.: [1] [2] [3]   **Rarity:** readily available ○

Calcite, red
Mineralogy: iron-containing calcium carbonate (trigonal, secondary)
Indications: (SP) for willpower **(S)** helps overcome laziness and listlessness **(M)** initiates competent and successful materialisation of ideas **(B)** promotes growth, fortifies immune system, stimulates blood clotting and wound healing and improves quality of the blood.
Bib.: [1] [2] [3]   **Rarity:** readily available ○

Calcite, yellow (Lemon Calcite)
Mineralogy: iron-containing calcium carbonate (trigonal, secondary)
Indications: (SP) self-esteem **(S)** fortifies sense of security, self-esteem and joie de vivre **(M)** makes resolute in disputes **(B)** stimulates food digestion, assimilation and metabolism; strengthens the skin, connective tissues, bones and teeth.
Bib.: [1] [2] [3]   **Rarity:** common ○

Carnelian, banded (Carnelian Agate)

Mineralogy: carnelian-coloured agate (quartz, trigonal, primary)
Indications: **(SP)** stimulates, motivates **(S)** helps overcome difficulties and energetically defend a cause **(M)** enhances receptivity **(B)** stimulates assimilation of vitamins, nutrients and minerals in the small intestine; improves blood viscosity.
Bib.: [1] [2] [3]   **Rarity:** not always available ○

Carnelian, orange

Mineralogy: chalcedony containing hematite (quartz, trig., prim.)
Indications: **(SP)** courage, willpower **(S)** gives vigour, courage, stability and good moods **(M)** promotes idealism, sense of community and pragmatism **(B)** improves quality of the blood; stimulates the small intestine, metabolism, circulation, blood flow.
Bib.: [1] [2] [3]   **Rarity:** not always available ○

Cassiterite

Mineralogy: tin oxide (rutile group, tetragonal, primary/tertiary)
Indications: **(SP)** greatness, perfection **(S)** promotes generosity in the right measure **(M)** helps realise dreams and perceive many things objectively **(B)** helps with eating disorders, emaciation or excess weight; has a regulating effect on the nerves and hormone system.
Bib.: [2]   **Rarity:** scarce ○

Cat's Eye Quartz (Aqualite, Schiller Quartz)

Mineralogy: quartz with hornblende fibre (trigonal/monoclinic, prim.)
Indications: **(SP)** insight, detachment **(S)** aids setting bounds and helps overcome great barriers at the same time **(M)** makes it easier to grasp complex contexts **(B)** relieves pain; calms the nerves; helps with hormonal hyperactivity.
Bib.: [2]   **Rarity:** not always available ○

Cavansite

Mineralogy: calcium vanadium sheet silicate (orthorh., prim.)
Indications: **(SP)** self-respect, sense of beauty **(S)** for encouragement and optimism, makes life-affirming **(M)** inspiration, learning ability, logical thinking **(B)** for cleansing and regeneration; helps with problems of the kidneys, bladder and ears (tinnitus).
Bib.: [2]   **Rarity:** scarce ○

Celestite
Mineralogy: strontium sulphate (orthorh, second./rarely prim.)
Indications: **(SP)** relief and stability **(S)** helps with severe feelings of constriction and unease and fainting fits **(M)** brings structure into one's life, thoughts and work **(B)** releases chronic tension and hardenings in bones, tissues and organs.
Bib.: [2]　　　　　　　　　　**Rarity:** readily available ○

Chalcedony, blue
Mineralogy: fibrous quartz (trigonal, primary/secondary)
Indications: **(SP)** presence of mind **(S)** helps accept new situations and overcome resistance **(M)** bestows inner calm and relaxed attention **(B)** stimulates milk production in nursing mothers; helps with sensitivity to weather changes; alleviates diabetes.
Bib.: [1] [2] [3]　　　　　　　**Rarity:** readily available ○

Chalcedony, blue banded (Blue Lace Agate)
Mineralogy: fibrous quartz (silicon dioxide, trigonal, primary)
Indications: **(SP)** communication **(S)** enhances rhetoric and self-expression **(M)** aids listening, understanding, confiding **(B)** promotes flow of lymph; helps thyroid gland, kidneys, bladder; with hoarseness, colds, allergies, blood pressure; fever-reducing effect.
Bib.: [1] [2] [3]　　　　　　　**Rarity:** Not always available ○

Chalcedony (Chrome Chalcedony)
Mineralogy: chalcedony containing chromium (quartz, trig., sec.)
Indications: **(SP)** carefree **(S)** bestows a light-hearted disposition to life; helps face up to worries and unpleasant matters **(M)** helps remain open to new ideas **(B)** has an anti-inflammatory effect, also on rheumatic diseases, polyarthritis among others.
Bib.: [1] [2]　　　　　　　　**Rarity:** not always available ○

Chalcedony (Copper Chalcedony)
Mineralogy: copper-containing chalcedony (trigonal, secondary)
Indications: **(SP)** for enjoyment, harmony **(S)** aids sensuality, openness and friendliness **(M)** promotes sense of judgement, tolerance, objective approach and sense of beauty **(B)** detoxifies; inhibits inflammations; helps with fungal infections; fortifies the immune system.
Bib.: [1] [2]　　　　　　　　**Rarity:** scarce ○

Chalcedony (Dendritic Chalcedony)

Mineralogy: chalcedony with manganese dendrites (trig., prim./sec.)
Indications: (SP) breaks habits (S) frees from unconscious habits, mechanisms and moods (M) aids precise thinking and attentive listening (B) activates cleansing of the lymph system, mucous membranes and respiratory tract; eases after-effects of smoking.
Bib.: [1] [2]   **Rarity:** readily available ○

Chalcedony, green

Mineralogy: chalcedony with iron silicates (trigonal, secondary)
Indications: (SP) forbearance, consideration (S) promotes a considerate attitude towards oneself and others (M) helps expend one's energy rationally (B) fortifies the immune reaction; improves wellbeing; helps with infections and enhances the senses.
Bib.: [1] [2]   **Rarity:** not always available ○

Chalcedony, pink (Rose Chalcedony)

Mineralogy: chalcedony containing manganese (quartz, trig., sec.)
Indications: (SP) for warm-heartedness (S) makes lively, kind and helpful (M) promotes openness and understanding (B) stimulates milk production in nursing mothers; helps with diabetes, colds and heart diseases caused by protracted infections.
Bib.: [1] [2] [3]   **Rarity:** readily available ○

Chalcedony, red (Blood Chalcedony)

Mineralogy: iron-containing chalcedony (quartz, trig., second.)
Indications: (SP) vigour, flexibility (S) enhances strength, vitality and vigour (M) fortifies willpower; keeps flexible whilst retaining one's standpoint (B) stabilises blood circulation, stimulates blood clotting and aids wound healing.
Bib.: [1] [2]   **Rarity:** readily available ○

Chalcedony, rosette

Mineralogy: petal-like chalcedony formations (trigonal, primary)
Indications: (SP) helps unfold (S) makes sociable and receptive (M) helps be oneself, express oneself clearly (B) helps problems of the stomach, skin, mucous membranes, respiratory tract, glands, tissues and sensory organs (depending on shape of petal-like formation).
Bib.: [1] [2] [3]   **Rarity:** readily available ○

Chalcedony, yellow (Carnelian yellow)
Mineralogy: chalcedony containing limonite (quartz, trig., prim.)
Indications: (SP) for modesty **(S)** makes content with very little, promotes contentment and joy **(M)** brings stability in thoughts and actions; helps find simple solutions **(B)** helps with weak circulation; aids digestion and elimination.
Bib.: [2] **Rarity:** readily available ○

Chalcopyrite
Mineralogy: copper iron sulphide (tetragonal, all formation stages)
Indications: (SP) curiosity, experience **(S)** exposes hidden causes of problems and illnesses **(M)** promotes the desire to understand life, improves power of observation and systematic thinking **(B)** promotes cleansing and excretion (intestine).
Bib.: [2] **Rarity:** readily available ○

Chalcopyrite Nephrite
Mineralogy: chalcopyrite nephrite mixture (tetrag./monocl., tert.)
Indications: (SP) for insight, experience **(S)** reveals one's less pleasant dark side; helps accept or change it **(M)** helps learn from mistakes **(B)** promotes cleansing/excretion through kidneys and intestines.
Bib.: [2] **Rarity:** scarce ○

Charoite
Mineralogy: sheet silicate rich in minerals (monoclinic, tertiary)
Indications: (SP) for vigour, determination **(S)** relaxes, helps overcome obsessions and obstacles **(M)** helps make important decisions and tackle huge piles of work **(B)** soothes the nerves, relieves pain and releases cramps.
Bib.: [1] [2] **Rarity:** not always available ○

Chiastolite
Mineralogy: aluminium island silicate with carbon (rhombic, tertiary)
Indications: (SP) identity, helps achieve one's vocation in life **(S)** helps overcome fear and feeling of guilt **(M)** promotes sense of reality and sobriety **(B)** alleviates hyperacidity, rheumatism and gout; helps with exhaustion, weakness and symptoms of paralysis.
Bib.: [1] [2] **Rarity:** scarce ○

Chloromelanite
Mineralogy: mixed diopside, jadeite, aegirine cryst. (monocl., tert.)
Indications: (SP) for balance, tolerance, carefulness (S) cures bad-temperedness, promotes wellbeing and trust (M) helps accept the unchangeable (B) relieves pain; strengthens the nerves; gives new energy and vitality; helps with kidney problems.
Bib.: [2]   **Rarity:** scarce ○

Chrome Diopside
Mineralogy: diopside containing chrome (chain silicate, monocl., tert.)
Indications: (SP) mental faculty, inspiration (S) helps face life in a carefree manner, makes lively and brings harmony and joie de vivre (M) promotes power of imagination and creativity (B) strengthens the kidneys, senses and nerves; ameliorates local inflammation.
Bib.: [2]   **Rarity:** scarce ○

Chrysoberyl
Mineralogy: aluminium beryllium oxide (orthorh, prim./tert.)
Indications: (SP) self-control, discipline (S) good for fear, feeling of unease, stress, nervousness, hyperactivity (M) promotes concentration, learning ability and strategic thinking (B) good for nerve problems, speech disorders, stammering and sensory disorders.
Bib.: [1] [2] [3]   **Rarity:** scarce ○

Chrysoberyl, Cat's Eye
Mineralogy: chrysoberyl with cat's eye (orthorhombic, tertiary)
Indications: (SP) self-determination, conviction (S) aids security, self-confidence and authority (M) helps stand firmly for one's conviction and convince others (B) strengthens the liver, brain, nerves, senses and immune system.
Bib.: [1] [2] [3]   **Rarity:** scarce ○

Chrysocolla
Mineralogy: hydrous copper ring silicate (monoclinic, secondary)
Indications: (SP) balance (S) good for stress and mood changes (M) helps keep one's cool (B) strengthens the liver; relaxes; helps with infections, sore throat, burns, scars, fever, cramps and menstrual pains.
Bib.: [1] [2] [3]   **Rarity:** readily available ○

Chrysocolla-Chalcedony (Gem Silica)
Mineralogy: chrysocolla in chalcedony (monocl./trig., second.)
Indications: (**SP**) sensitivity (**S**) alleviates nervousness and irritability (**M**) refines perception, enhances sense of beauty (**B**) excites the senses; helps with infections, fever and cramps; aids detoxification, liver and kidneys; reduces fever and blood pressure.
Bib.: [2]   **Rarity:** rare ○

Chrysoprase
Mineralogy: chalcedony containing nickel (quartz, trig., second.)
Indications: (**SP**) detoxification (**S**) promotes trust, and sense of safety; helps with heartache, jealousy and nightmares (**M**) helps solve relationship problems (**B**) purifies, detoxifies, and helps with allergies, epilepsy, skin diseases, fungal infections and rheumatism.
Bib.: [1] [2] [3]   **Rarity:** readily available ○

Cinnabar (Cinnabarite)
Mineralogy: mercury sulphide (trigonal, primary/rarely secondary)
Indications: (**SP**) uncompromising (**S**) helps with instability, restlessness and nervousness (**M**) eases concentration problems (**B**) helps with indurate glands and diseases of the intestine, skin and mucous membranes. **Caution:** may contain metallic mercury – poisonous!
Bib.: [2]   **Rarity:** scarce ○

Cinnabar Opal
Mineralogy: opal with cinnabar inclusions (amorphous/trig., prim.)
Indications: (**SP**) deep cleansing (**S**) helps transform stubborn destructive patterns (**M**) makes flexible, capable of learning (**B**) detoxifies intensively right down to elimination of heavy metals (NB often with strong initial reactions); helps with tonsillitis and inflammation.
Bib.: –   **Rarity:** rare ○

Citrine
Mineralogy: yellow crystal quartz (silicon dioxide, trigonal, primary)
Indications: (**SP**) gives courage to face life (**S**) gives joie de vivre; aids self-expression; helps with depression (**M**) helps deal with and understand absorbed impressions (**B**) fortifies the nerves, stomach, spleen and pancreas; also helps with bedwetting.
Bib.: [1] [2] [3]   **Rarity:** not always available ○

Conglomerate

Mineralogy: coarse grainy sediment (diverse structures, secondary)
Indications: (SP) critical thinking and correction (S) improves one's sense of enhancing or hindering influences (M) helps scrutinise oneself now and again and correct one's desires (B) fortifies circulation, the spleen, small intestine and digestion.
Bib.: [2]   Rarity: not always available ○

Conglomerate with Pyrite

Mineralogy: pyrite quartz rock (cubic/trigonal, secondary)
Indications: (SP) self-assessment, self-recognition (S) helps confront one's dark side (M) improves the assessment of one's energy and abilities (B) stimulates intensive purification and elimination processes.
Bib.: [2]   Rarity: scarce ○

Copper

Mineralogy: precious metal (natural element, cubic, secondary)
Indications: (SP) beauty (S) promotes sense of aesthetic, harmony and love for all beings (M) lends playful creativity and promotes sense of justice (B) for fertility; eases cramps and menstrual pains; fortifies the liver and brain.
Bib.: [2]   Rarity: readily available ○

Cordierite (Iolite, Dichroite)

Mineralogy: aluminium ring silicate (orthorhombic, tertiary)
Indications: (SP) firmness (S) self-assurance; endurance in adverse situations (M) helps take on responsibility and fulfil duties (B) strengthens the nerves, helps with paralysis and numb limbs, and bearing pain.
Bib.: [2]   Rarity: readily available ○

Cordierite (Iolite Sunstone)

Mineralogy: cordierite with hematite inclusions (orthorh., tert.)
Indications: (SP) willpower (S) hope in difficult situations (M) aids ability to draw spiritual benefit from defeats (B) releases cramps, boosts performance, stabilises the circulation and helps with fainting fits.
Bib.: –   Rarity: scarce ○

Covellite

Mineralogy: blue (wet violet) copper sulphide (hex., second.)
Indications: (SP) self-love, self-recognition (S) helps with discontentment, arrogance and vanity (M) helps accept oneself as one is (B) improves feeling of wellbeing; harmonises stress and rest; promotes digestion, detoxification and sexuality.
Bib.: [2]   **Rarity:** scarce ○

Danburite

Mineralogy: calcium boron lattice silicate (rhomb., prim./rarely tert.)
Indications: (SP) for selflessness, spiritual orientation (S) self-acceptance, unconditional love (M) releases constraining behavioural patterns (B) helps with problems of the heart, circulation and digestion with underlying emotional causes, including anorexia.
Bib.: [2]   **Rarity:** not always available ○

Diamond

Mineralogy: pure carbon (natural element, cubic, tertiary)
Indications: (SP) invincible (S) promotes strength of character, ethics and faithfulness to oneself (M) makes responsible and objective (B) purifies and strengthens the brain, nerves, sensory organs, glands and blood vessels, good for strokes.
Bib.: [1] [2] [3]   **Rarity:** readily available ○

Diaspor

Mineralogy: aluminium oxy-hydroxide (orthorhombic, tertiary)
Indications: (SP) revives original objectives (S) for perception and change of relationship structures (M) triggers self-analysis and change of one's life (B) promotes digestion, de-acidifies and helps with heartburn and stomach problems.
Bib.: [3]   **Rarity:** scarce ○

Diopside

Mineralogy: chain silicate of the pyroxene group (monocl., tertiary)
Indications: (SP) forgiveness, letting go (S) helps let go of old pains and wounds (M) helps approach others and make peace (B) aids the kidneys and regulates the hormone, acid-base, mineral and water balance.
Bib.: [2]   **Rarity:** not always available ○

Diopside (Star diopside)
Mineralogy: chain silicate of the pyroxene group (monocl., tertiary)
Indications: (SP) for spirituality (S) harmonises extreme mood changes (M) aids the recognition of the spiritual nature of being and the underlying spiritual causes of all phenomena (B) fortifies the heart, kidneys, nerves, muscles and blood vessels.
Bib.: [2]   **Rarity:** scarce ○

Dioptase
Mineralogy: hydrous copper ring silicate (trigonal, secondary)
Indications: (SP) for wealth, beauty, happiness (S) helps project one-self in the right light, bestows depth of feeling, hope and intensive dreams (M) helps tap into one's potentials, brings a wealth of ideas and creativity (B) fortifies the liver, alleviates pain and cramps.
Bib.: [1] [2]   **Rarity:** scarce ○

Disthene, blue (Cyanite, Kyanite)
Mineralogy: blue aluminium island silicate (triclinic, tertiary)
Indications: (SP) identity, life-fulfilling vocation (S) helps remain func-tional in extreme situations (M) promotes a logical way of thinking and resolute action (B) alleviates hoarseness and problems of the larynx; good for the motor nerves and dexterity.
Bib.: [1] [2]   **Rarity:** not always available ○

Disthene, green
Mineralogy: green aluminium island silicate (triclinic, tertiary)
Indications: (SP) identity, instinct (S) helps overcome victimhood and resignation (M) overcomes fatalistic attitude and promotes a sure instinctive action (B) alleviates hyperacidity, rheumatism and gout; aids mobility; good for the motor nerves and dexterity.
Bib.: [1] [2]   **Rarity:** rare ○

Dolomite, banded
Mineralogy: dolomite with stripes containing iron (trig., second.)
Indications: (SP) talent (S) ensures stability and helps with sudden and weighty emotional outbursts (M) aids development of personal abilities (B) alleviates stiff muscles and has a cramp releasing effect, good for the blood, heart, circulation and blood vessels.
Bib.: [1] [2]   **Rarity:** readily available ○

Dolomite, beige (Ivorite)
Mineralogy: calcium magnesium carbonate (trigonal, secondary)
Indications: (SP) calmness **(S)** relaxes; lends patience and inner contentment **(M)** promotes simple pragmatic thinking and helps tackle problems calmly **(B)** alleviates headaches and reduces deposits in the blood vessels and predispositions to thrombosis.
Bib.: [1] [2]   Rarity: readily available ○

Dolomite, orange
Mineralogy: dolomite containing iron (trigonal, secondary)
Indications: (SP) joy **(S)** has an restorative and encouraging effect, stabilises constant mood changes **(M)** aids discovery of personal abilities **(B)** stimulates circulation, digestion and metabolism; strengthens the heart in times of great strain.
Bib.: [1] [2]   Rarity: rare ○

Dolomite with Pyrite
Mineralogy: dolomite with pyrite layers (trigonal/cubic, secondary)
Indications: (SP) talent **(S)** helps convert weaknesses into strengths and redress misunderstandings **(M)** aids discovery of personal abilities **(B)** enhances detoxification, deacidification and excretion; helps with problems of the stomach and intestine.
Bib.: [1] [2]   Rarity: readily available ○

Dolomite, white (Sugar Dolomite)
Mineralogy: calcium magnesium carbonate (trigonal, secondary)
Indications: (SP) self-discovery **(S)** brings balance and stability **(M)** enhances commonsense; helps achieve personal aims easily and simply **(B)** relaxes; detoxifies; keeps vital and healthy; relieves pain and releases cramps.
Bib.: [1] [2]   Rarity: readily available ○

Dumortierite
Mineralogy: aluminium boron silicate (island silicate, orthorh., prim.)
Indications: (SP) detachment **(S)** helps take life lightly and alleviates fear, depression, nervousness and stress **(M)** helps overcome obsessive behavioural patterns (addiction) **(B)** alleviates headaches, cramps, diarrhoea, nausea and vomiting.
Bib.: [1] [2] [3]   Rarity: readily available ○

Eclogite

Mineralogy: rock with pyroxene and garnet (diverse structures, tertiary)

Indications: (SP) recovery **(S)** brings hope in difficult phases of life; aids the will to recover **(M)** dissipates fixed ideas of bad luck, danger and failure **(B)** stimulates regeneration and self-healing power; helps with severe and protracted diseases.

Bib.: [2]   **Rarity:** not always available ○

Eilatstone (Chrysocolla-Malachite-Turquoise)

Mineralogy: mixture of copper minerals (monocl./tricl., sec.)

Indications: (SP) sense of beauty **(S)** promotes a lively, eventful and harmonious emotional life **(M)** gives a fine sense of beauty and harmony **(B)** fortifies the liver; regulates disharmonious cell growth; alleviates menstrual pains.

Bib.: [2]   **Rarity:** rare ○

Eldarite (Nebula stone)

Mineralogy: quartz anorthoclase riebeckite aegirine vulcanite (primary)

Indications: (SP) integration, vigour, protection **(S)** overcomes strain, fear, negativity and external influence **(M)** clears doubts and worries; makes conscious suppressed personal interests **(B)** enhances the function of the skin, sweat glands and body fluids.

Bib.: –   **Rarity:** rare ○

Emerald

Mineralogy: beryl cont. chromium (ring silicate, hexag., prim./tert.)

Indications: (SP) seeking meaning **(S)** promotes harmony and justice; recuperation and regeneration **(M)** supports seeking and realising objectives **(B)** helps with sinusitis, headaches, epilepsy, and diseases of the eyes, heart and intestine.

Bib.: [1] [2] [3]   **Rarity:** readily available ○

Emerald in Matrix

Mineralogy: emerald embedded in quartzite (hexagonal/trig., tert.)

Indications: (SP) orientation **(S)** helps come to terms with blows of fate **(M)** helps find new orientation in times of crises **(B)** strengthens the liver, detoxifies, de-acidifies and helps with colds, infections, inflammations, rheumatism and gout.

Bib.: [1] [2] [3]   **Rarity:** not always available ○

Epidote
Mineralogy: calcium aluminium group silicate (monoclinic, primary)
Indications: (SP) regeneration **(S)** brings patience, dissipates anxiety, self-pity and grief **(M)** helps realise one's idea of happiness and fulfilment **(B)** fortifies the liver, gallbladder and digestive system; regenerates after over-exertion or illness.
Bib.: [1] [2] [3]   **Rarity:** not always available ○

Epidote Feldspar (Snowflake Epidote)
Mineralogy: epidote feldspar mixture (monoclinic, primary/tertiary)
Indications: (SP) regeneration **(S)** helps deal with after-effects of strain or painful experiences **(M)** teaches not to over-exert oneself **(B)** fortifies the liver and gallbladder; aids regeneration and recovery, especially when major weaknesses have an obstructive effect.
Bib.: [1] [2] [3]   **Rarity:** scarce ○

Epidote Feldspar (Unakite)
Mineralogy: epidote feldspar mixture (monoclinic, primary/tertiary)
Indications: (SP) recovery **(S)** builds up and strengthens; helps overcome frustrations caused by setbacks **(M)** teaches not to derogate oneself because of mistakes **(B)** fortifies the liver and gallbladder; enhances power of regeneration and accelerates healing processes.
Bib.: [1] [2] [3]   **Rarity:** common ○

Epidote Quartz
Mineralogy: epidote needles in quartz (trigonal/monoclinic, primary)
Indications: (SP) fresh impetus **(S)** gives courage, and hope after great disappointments **(M)** improves performance and discerning ability **(B)** rejuvenates quickly; relieves pain and helps with bruises and sprains.
Bib.: [2]   **Rarity:** scarce ○

Eudialyte
Mineralogy: alkaline ring silicate rich in minerals (trigonal, primary)
Indications: (SP) turning point, new orientation **(S)** helps overcome grief, fear and pain, accept personal weaknesses **(M)** for new beginnings, learning from mistakes, overcoming resistance **(B)** refills energy reserves after complete over-exertion.
Bib.: [2]   **Rarity:** scarce ○

Falcon's Eye (blue Tiger's Eye)
Mineralogy: bluish-black fibrous quartz (trigonal, primary)
Indications: (SP) overview, reserve (S) helps with nervousness and inner restlessness (M) makes it easy to retain overview in complex situations and helps with difficulties in decision making (B) relieves pain; helps with shivering, and hormonal hyperactivity.
Bib.: [1] [2]   **Rarity:** common ○

Feldspar (Multicoloured Feldspar)
Mineralogy: mixture of different feldspars (monocl./tricl., primary)
Indications: (SP) eagerness to learn, flexibility (S) feeling of wellbeing, balance, promotes interest in life itself (M) broadens the perceptive faculty; makes new approaches possible (B) good for problems of the spleen, pancreas, stomach, intestine and gallbladder.
Bib.: [2]   **Rarity:** not always available ○

Fire Opal
Mineralogy: red to yellow precious opal containing iron (amorph., prim.)
Indications: (SP) zest for life, enjoyment (S) makes impulsive, helps overcome inhibitions, aids enjoyment of sexuality (M) awakens enthusiasm for interesting ideas (B) enhances energy, performance, circulation, blood flow, virility and fertility.
Bib.: [1] [2] [3]   **Rarity:** not always available ○

Flint (Firestone)
Mineralogy: chalcedony and opal mixture (trig./amorph., second.)
Indications: (SP) for understanding (S) calms, for composure (M) makes communicative and promotes listening abilities (B) fortifies function of the mucous membranes, lungs, skin and intestine; improves detoxification, helps with constipation and diarrhoea.
Bib.: [2]   **Rarity:** readily available ○

Fluorite, blue
Mineralogy: calcium fluoride (halide, cubic, mostly primary)
Indications: (SP) interest, justice (S) makes sober and quiet, helps with frustration and disappointment (M) helps release obsessions and aids sense of justice (B) alleviates cough and hoarseness; helps with posture damage, deformities; bony growth or swelling.
Bib.: [1] [2] [3]   **Rarity:** readily available ○

Fluorite, green

Mineralogy: calcium fluoride (halide, cubic, mostly primary)

Indications: (SP) aids creativity and dissolves blockages **(S)** intensifies emotions and moods, making them obvious **(M)** overcomes narrow-mindedness; brings ideas and a quick intellectual grasp **(B)** aids detox-ification; helps with arthritis, rheumatism, gout and fungal infections.

Bib.: [1] [2] [3] **Rarity:** readily available ○

Fluorite, multicoloured (Rainbow fluorite)

Mineralogy: multicoloured fluorite (halide, cubic, primary)

Indications: (SP) freethinkingness, flexibility **(S)** brings variety and emotional liveliness **(M)** aids freedom of choice and makes inventive **(B)** good for the skin, mucous membranes, nerves, bones and teeth; alleviates dry cough, makes joints flexible.

Bib.: [1] [2] [3] **Rarity:** readily available ○

Fluorite Opal Jasper

Mineralogy: fluorite opal jasper mixture (cub./amorph./trig., sec.)

Indications: (SP) light-hearted freedom **(S)** intuition, effortlessness, gentleness, relieves extreme tensions **(M)** for living in the present; makes inventive and objective **(B)** helps with allergies, lymph block-ages, problems of the skin and respiratory tract, infections, cough.

Bib.: – **Rarity:** rare ○

Fluorite, pink

Mineralogy: calcium fluoride (halide, cubic, primary)

Indications: (SP) for goodwill; makes dynamic **(S)** helps perceive and express suppressed emotions **(M)** makes active, open and good-natured **(B)** alleviates functional heart problems; aids hormone regu-lation; helps with osteoporosis.

Bib.: [1] [2] [3] **Rarity:** rare ○

Fluorite, violet

Mineralogy: calcium fluoride (halide, cubic, mostly primary)

Indications: (SP) liberation, self-determination **(S)** for emotional sta-bility and inner peace **(M)** helps with learning and concentrating dis-orders, fortifies the memory **(B)** helps with overweight caused by wrong eating habits, with tumours and septic wounds.

Bib.: [1] [2] [3] **Rarity:** readily available ○

Fluorite, white
Mineralogy: calcium fluoride (halide, cubic, mostly primary)
Indications: (SP) order, purification (S) helps with feelings of guilt and impurity, makes more emotionally stable (M) clears confusion and helps maintain order (B) good for the skin, mucous membranes, respiratory tract, nerves and brain; alleviates cough and allergies.
Bib.: [1] [2] [3]   **Rarity:** readily available ○

Fluorite, yellow
Mineralogy: calcium fluoride (halide, cubic, mostly primary)
Indications: (SP) learning, understanding (S) promotes a positive attitude to life (M) helps digest information and experiences faster (B) helps with stomach problems and eating disorders (including anorexia); fortifies bones and joints.
Bib.: [1] [2] [3]   **Rarity:** readily available ○

Fuchsite
Mineralogy: chrome mica (sheet silicate, monoclinic, mostly tertiary)
Indications: (SP) protection, self-determination (S) helps set boundaries; aids a confident and convincing appearance; (M) helps view problems from a distance, thus finding solutions (B) helps with allergies, itching, inflammation and effects of rays.
Bib.: [2]   **Rarity:** readily available ○

Fuchsite Kyanite
Mineralogy: fuchsite and kyanite mixture (monocl./tricl., tert.)
Indications: (SP) integrity, individuality (S) helps remain independent even under pressure; removes fear of losing mental faculties (M) helps avoid injuries (B) helps with roving pain; alleviates inflammations; good for the nerves and skin.
Bib.: –   **Rarity:** scarce ○

Gabbro (Blackstone)
Mineralogy: plutonite poor in silicic acid (diverse structures, primary)
Indications: (SP) for new beginnings (S) fortifies in times of exhausting routines; aids listening to oneself and perceiving one's needs (M) helps plan and prepare new steps carefully (B) fortifies the regenerating and self-healing power.
Bib.: [2]   **Rarity:** not always available ○

Galaxyite (Labradorite rock)
Mineralogy: labradorite/amphibole mixture (tricl./monocl., prim.)
Indications: (SP) helps emotional depth, striving for fulfilment (S) aids deep sleep with good dream recall (M) helps constructively combine compassion, clarity and sense of reality (B) calms the heartbeat and circulation and aids the function of the kidneys.
Bib.: [2]   **Rarity:** scarce ○

Galena (Lead glance)
Mineralogy: grey lead sulphide (cubic, all formation stages)
Indications: (SP) severity, calm, coming to terms with inner void (S) calms disposition, helps overcome melancholy (M) turns away thoughts from the past; sobriety (B) detoxification; dissolves deposits in the joints; helps with stiffness and immobility.
Bib.: [2]   **Rarity:** readily available ○

Garnet Almandine
Mineralogy: iron aluminium island silicate (cubic, tertiary)
Indications: (SP) increases powers of resistance (S) fortifies willpower and helps live one's sexuality (M) aids insight and helps achieve one's ideas against great resistance (B) makes active and stimulates circulation, blood building and metabolism.
Bib.: [1] [2]   **Rarity:** readily available ○

Garnet Andradite
Mineralogy: calcium iron island silicate (cubic, tertiary)
Indications: (SP) willpower, orientation (S) for intuition, safety and trust (M) enhances creativity, shrewdness and flexibility (B) stimulates the liver and blood building; improves vitality, mobility and fitness; helps with missed menstruation.
Bib.: [1] [2]: [Variety Demantoide]   **Rarity:** scarce ○

Garnet Chrome Grossular
Mineralogy: grossular containing chrome (island silicate, cubic, tertiary)
Indications: (SP) restorative; aids self-determination (S) brings new drive in times of stagnation (M) revives imagination and creativity (B) fortifies the liver and kidneys; detoxifies and alleviates inflammations; regulates fat metabolism, prevents arteriosclerosis.
Bib.: [2]   **Rarity:** scarce ○

Garnet Grossular

Mineralogy: calcium aluminium island silicate (cubic, tertiary)
Indications: (SP) restorative; regeneration (S) brings hope and readiness to co-operate with others (M) helps develop new perspectives (B) fortifies liver and kidney; helps with rheumatism and arthritis; detoxifies/regenerates the skin and mucous membranes.
Bib.: [1] [2]   Rarity: not always available ○

Garnet Grossularite

Mineralogy: rock containing grossular (mostly cubic, tertiary)
Indications: (SP) restorative; fosters community spirit (S) promotes social unity in difficult times (M) helps formulate new ideas and express them (B) fortifies the liver and kidneys; helps with rheumatism and arthritis; detoxifies and regenerates the skin and mucous membranes.
Bib.: [1] [2]   Rarity: readily available ○

Garnet Hessonite

Mineralogy: grossular containing iron (island silicate, cubic, tertiary)
Indications: (SP) self-respect; restorative; growth (S) soothes emotional agitation, brings clarity into emotions (M) helps appreciate one's abilities (B) fortifies the liver and kidneys; regulates the hormone balance in cases of hyper and hypo function of glands.
Bib.: [1] [2]   Rarity: scarce ○

Garnet Hydrogrossular

Mineralogy: hydrous grossularite (island silicate, cubic, tertiary)
Indications: (SP) restorative; helps amendment, order (S) brings emotional engagement, dissipates self-pity (M) replaces wrong ideas with a realistic view (B) fortifies the kidneys, liver and gallbladder; aids detoxification and elimination.
Bib.: –   Rarity: scarce ○

Garnet in Matrix (Almandine)

Mineralogy: almandine in mica slate (diverse structures, tertiary)
Indications: (SP) willpower, fitness, capacity for work (S) gives strength to master great difficulties (M) gives vigour to carry out ideas and duties (B) boosts performance, stimulates metabolism and promotes detoxification and excretion at the same time.
Bib.: [1] [2]   Rarity: readily available ○

Garnet Melanite
Mineralogy: Andradite cont. titanium (island silicate, cubic, tertiary)
Indications: (SP) self-discovery, sincerity **(S)** for reliability, stability and trust **(M)** makes more receptive to one's conscience and strengthens 'resistance' in disputes **(B)** promotes growth in height and fortifies the bones and spine.
Bib.: [1] [2] **Rarity:** scarce ○

Garnet Pyrope
Mineralogy: magnesium aluminium island silicate (cubic, tertiary)
Indications: (SP) crisis management; quality of life **(S)** promotes composure, courage and endurance; dissipates awkwardness; stimulates sexuality **(M)** supports the striving for improvement **(B)** enhances blood quality and blood flow; helps with bladder problems.
Bib.: [1] [2] [3] **Rarity:** not always available ○

Garnet Rhodolite
Mineralogy: pyrope-almandine crystal (island silicate, cubic, tertiary)
Indications: (SP) optimism, zest for life, charisma **(S)** promotes trust, warm-heartedness, sexuality and sensuality; boosts virility **(M)** helps face challenges with optimism **(B)** stimulates circulation and metabolism, improves blood flow.
Bib.: [1] [2] **Rarity:** scarce ○

Garnet Spessartine
Mineralogy: manganese-aluminium island silicate (cub./ tert./ prim.)
Indications: (SP) determination, helpfulness **(S)** helps with nightmares, depression and sexual problems **(M)** helps talk about and clear oppressing and embarrassing things regarded as taboos **(B)** fortifies the heart, small intestine (assimilation) and immune system.
Bib.: [1] [2] **Rarity:** scarce ○

Garnet Tsavorite
Mineralogy: grossular containing chrome and vanadium (cub., tert.)
Indications: (SP) restorative, freeing **(S)** brings new strength in difficult phases of life **(M)** helps one break through paralysing problems **(B)** detoxifies and helps with inflammation as well as with protracted, chronic and degenerative diseases.
Bib.: [2] **Rarity:** rare ○

Garnet Uvarovite
Mineralogy: calcium chrome island silicate (cubic, tertiary)
Indications: (SP) individuality, independence **(S)** makes enquiring and optimistic **(M)** brings enthusiasm and vigour for one's ideas **(B)** fortifies the pancreas, aids detoxification and has an anti-inflammatory and fever-enhancing effect (when necessary).
Bib.: [1] [2]   **Rarity:** rare ○

Gaspeite
Mineralogy: nickel carbonate containing magnesium (trig., second.)
Indications: (SP) life-affirming **(S)** peps up, makes jovial, aids benevolence and agility **(M)** self-critical, makes quick-witted enough to recognise pranks played by self or others **(B)** helpful for detoxification and over-acidity (with chalcedony for elimination).
Bib.: [2]   **Rarity:** scarce ○

Girasol (Opal Chalcedony)
Mineralogy: opal/chalcedony mixture (amorph./trig., prim.)
Indications: (SP) for solutions, freedom **(S)** clears unrest, discontentment and longing by revealing hidden feelings and impressions influencing the mind **(M)** makes conscious of wishes and needs **(B)** releases tension, hardenings and swellings of the lymph nodes.
Bib.: [2]   **Rarity:** scarce ○

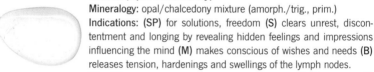

Girasol Quartz (Moon Quartz, Foggy Quartz)
Mineralogy: rock crystal clouded by water/rutile (trig., prim.)
Indications: (SP) clarification, independence **(S)** makes calm, balanced, open, able to cope with strain, aids problem solving through dream **(M)** improves perception and overview; promotes clear, quick, precise thinking **(B)** activates and cures latent illnesses.
Bib.: [2]   **Rarity:** not always available ○

Glass (natural)
Mineralogy: solidified silicon dioxide molten glass (amorph., prim.)
Indications: (SP) cheerfulness, fun **(S)** makes spontaneous, impulsive and sociable, gives joie de vivre **(M)** helps give up doubts and allow diverse views **(B)** helps with clouding of the eyeball and lenses (cataracts); good for the stomach and pancreas.
Bib.: [2]   **Rarity:** scarce ○

Glauconite in Sandstone

Mineralogy: green sheet silicate in sandstone (monocl., second.)

Indications: (SP) contentment, serenity (S) brings calm and contentment (M) aids relaxed detachment (B) promotes cleansing of the connective tissues; fortifies the immune system; alleviates allergic reactions.

Bib.: –   **Rarity:** not always available ○

Glaucophane with Garnet

Mineralogy: amphibole rock with garnet (monoclinic/cubic, tertiary)

Indications: (SP) transformation, freedom (S) helps face up to unpleasant issues, live out emotions, resolve conflicts (M) aids clearing misunderstandings, makes self-aware (B) fortifies perception of one's body, senses and circulation; helps release tensions.

Bib.: –   **Rarity:** scarce ○

Gneiss

Mineralogy: layered metamorphic rock rich in mica (tertiary)

Indications: (SP) for upheaval, transition (S) aids facing up to unpleasant situations, to endure until transformation sets in (M) helps recognise and give up habits and unhelpful tendencies (B) promotes digestion and excretion.

Bib.: [2]   **Rarity:** readily available ○

Goethite quartz (Cacoxenite)

Mineralogy: crystal quartz containing goethite (orthorh./trig., prim.)

Indications: (SP) carefreeness (S) alleviates fear, constrictions and inhibitions (M) helps distract thoughts from (present) unsolvable problems (B) helps with cough, colds, 'flu and infections of the respiratory tract right down to inflammation of the lungs.

Bib.: [2]   **Rarity:** scarce ○

Gold

Mineralogy: golden precious metal (cubic, all formation stages)

Indications: (SP) gives a sheen (S) helps with discontentment, inferiority complex and depression (M) helps see the 'positive' aspect of things thus making them easier to bear (B) regulates the glands, nerves and circulation; has a warming effect; fortifies the sexual organs.

Bib.: [2]   **Rarity:** scarce ○

Gold Beryl

Mineralogy: gold-yellow beryl (ring silicate, hexagonal, primary)
Indications: (SP) optimism (S) brings hope and joie de vivre, alleviates irritability and nervousness, relief from heavy burdens (M) helps accept the unchangeable and improve on the changeable (B) fortifies the nerves, eyes, stomach, spleen and pancreas.
Bib.: [1] [2]   **Rarity:** rare ○

Gold Quartz (Tiger's eye Quartz)

Mineralogy: tiger's eye with high amount of quartz (trig., second.)
Indications: (SP) helps assert oneself (S) helps withstand difficulties without losing courage (M) helps digest impressions and concentrate on fundamentals (B) releases tension and helps with acute asthma attacks.
Bib.: [2] [3]   **Rarity:** scarce ○

Granite

Mineralogy: magmatite with feldspar quartz and mica (primary)
Indications: (SP) tradition, stabilisation (S) helps draw strength and might from one's experiences, roots and traditional origins (M) firms up new ideas and gives form and strength for sure realisation (B) stimulates the heart and circulation; animates and vitalises.
Bib.: [1] [2]   **Rarity:** readily available ○

Gwindel Quartz (Quartz Gwindel)

Mineralogy: conjoined quartz crystals with slight twist (trig., prim.)
Indications: (SP) orientation, transformation (S) clears confusion and uncertainty (M) helps cope with complicated situations (B) mobilises and controls energy flow, dissipates tension, alleviates cramps, general pain and back pain.
Bib.: [1]   **Rarity:** rare ○

Halite (Salt Stone, Salt Crystal)

Mineralogy: sodium chloride (halide, cubic, secondary)
Indications: (SP) protection, purification (S) makes lively and brings inner balance (M) dissolves unconscious thought and behavioural patterns (B) regulates metabolism and water balance; eliminates, detoxifies, cleanses and protects the respiratory tract, intestine and skin.
Bib.: [2]   **Rarity:** common ○

Heliodor
Mineralogy: yellowish green beryl (ring silicate, hexagonal, primary)
Indications: (SP) resistance, stability **(S)** helps bear immense pressure (internal and external); reduces aggressiveness **(M)** helps plan in advance while still remaining flexible **(B)** strengthens the immune system and helps with short- and long-sightedness.
Bib.: [1] [2]   **Rarity:** scarce ○

Heliotrope (Bloodstone)
Mineralogy: green jasper with red spots (trigonal, secondary)
Indications: (SP) immune protection **(S)** aids setting bounds **(M)** helps maintain control **(B)** fortifies the lymph and immune reaction; helps with problems of the heart, blood vessels and bladder as well as with 'flu, colds, infections, inflammation and pus formation.
Bib.: [1] [2] [3]   **Rarity:** common ○

Hematite banded (Banded Iron Ore)
Mineralogy: iron oxide (trigonal, as banded iron ore secondary)
Indications: (SP) strength, endurance **(S)** fortifies staying power during intensive work or exertion **(M)** helps realise one's plans in spite of obstacles **(B)** promotes iron assimilation, blood building and oxygen transport; fortifies the liver, spleen and intestine.
Bib.: [1] [2] [3]   **Rarity:** not always available ○

Hematite (Kidney Growth, Red Glass Head)
Mineralogy: iron oxide (trigonal, as red glass head primary)
Indications: (SP) survival **(S)** fortifies willpower and brings unfulfilled wishes to light **(M)** directs attention to basic needs and physical well-being **(B)** promotes iron assimilation and blood building; fortifies the small and large intestines and kidneys.
Bib.: [1] [2] [3]   **Rarity:** not always available ○

Hematite with Magnetite
Mineralogy: iron oxide (trigonal/cubic, coarse tertiary rock)
Indications: (SP) progress, engagement **(S)** promotes striving for improvement of one's situation in life **(M)** helps pursue aims with determination and to fight for them if necessary **(B)** aids assimilation of iron and blood building, stimulates the glands, liver and gallbladder.
Bib.: [1] [2] [3]   **Rarity:** common ○

Hematite Quartz
Mineralogy: hematite platelets in crystal quartz (trigonal, primary)
Indications: (SP) vitality **(S)** strengthens, rejuvenates, cheers up, enhances courage and enthusiasm **(M)** helps properly apportion one's energy in spiritual and physical exertions **(B)** enhances blood building, stabilises circulation, fortifies the muscles, nerves and senses.
Bib.: [2]   **Rarity:** rare ○

Hemimorphite
Mineralogy: alkaline zinc group silicate (orthorhombic, secondary)
Indications: (SP) helps adjust to one's goal **(S)** bestows a calm peaceful nature **(M)** helps recognise external influences **(B)** generally restorative; helps with heart problems, warts, sunburn, burns, for wound healing and restless legs.
Bib.: [2]   **Rarity:** scarce ○

Hermanov Ball (Phlogopite Anthophyllite)
Mineralogy: phlogopite in anthophyllite (monocl/orthorh, tertiary)
Indications: (SP) trust, innocence, protection **(S)** bestows a positive disposition to life, helps retain a soft core under an external hard shell **(M)** ends self-doubt and agonising brooding **(B)** detoxifies and regulates the function of the kidneys and gonads.
Bib.: [2]   **Rarity:** rare ○

Heulandite
Mineralogy: zeolite leaves (lattice silicate, monoclinic, primary)
Indications: (SP) mobility **(S)** helps give up negative emotions **(M)** makes changing habits easier **(B)** fortifies the kidneys and liver; promotes blood flow; good for mobility, joints, discs, knee (meniscus) and feet.
Bib.: [2]   **Rarity:** not always available ○

Hiddenite (Spodumene)
Mineralogy: yellowish-green chain silicate (pyroxene, monocl., prim.)
Indications: (SP) devotion **(S)** teaches devotion without self-denial **(M)** improves memory, helps with difficulties in decision making **(B)** alleviates problems of the joints; helps with nervous diseases, neuralgia, sciatic neuralgia and toothache.
Bib.: [2]   **Rarity:** scarce ○

Hornblende

Mineralogy: chain silicate (amphibole group, monocl., prim./tert.)
Indications: (SP) unity, integration **(S)** helps dissipate inner conflict and obsessive strain **(M)** helps cope with contrasts by allowing each aspect its necessary space **(B)** good for the small intestine and kidneys as well as for middle and inner ear problems.
Bib.: [2]   **Rarity:** readily available ○

Hornstone, brown

Mineralogy: jasper opal mixture (trigonal/amorphous, secondary)
Indications: (SP) productivity **(S)** reduces stress, makes relaxed, brings gentle surge of energy **(M)** helps realise plans in a simple way **(B)** purifies connective tissues and skin; alleviates allergies; improves intestinal flora and helps with constipation and diarrhoea.
Bib.: [2]   **Rarity:** readily available ○

Hornstone, coloured (Flint coloured)

Mineralogy: jasper opal mixture (trigonal/amorphous, secondary)
Indications: (SP) exchange, open-mindedness **(S)** flexibility and composure **(M)** promotes team spirit **(B)** purifies connective tissues and skin; good against corns and swellings; enhances stability of the vessels, digestion and elimination.
Bib.: [2]   **Rarity:** not always available ○

Howlite

Mineralogy: calcium boron silicate (island silicate, monocl., second.)
Indications: (SP) independence, care **(S)** aids taking control of one's life **(M)** promotes conscious control of one's actions **(B)** fortifies sense of balance; helps with nausea, eases vomiting; ameliorates skin irritation caused by contact poison.
Bib.: [2]   **Rarity:** scarce ○

Hypersthene

Mineralogy: glittering chain silicate (pyroxene, orthorh., prim.)
Indications: (SP) balance **(S)** brings right measure of activity and rest; makes dynamic and emotionally balanced **(M)** helps accept criticism and defend one's conviction **(B)** eases tension, relieves pain and helps with hyperacidity.
Bib.: [2] [6]   **Rarity:** scarce ○

Ilmenite Quartz
Mineralogy: ilmenite needles in quartz (oxide, trigonal, primary)
Indications: **(SP)** inspiration, image **(S)** accentuates personality, character and abilities **(M)** helps differentiate between inspiration and illusion and to attempt great deeds **(B)** helps with signs of constriction, degeneration or wear and tear.
Bib.: [2]   Rarity: scarce ○

Iron Nickel Meteorite
Mineralogy: iron nickel alloy (cubic, interplanetary formation)
Indications: **(SP)** aids crosschecking personal intentions and aims **(S)** releases inner images, renews outdated structures **(M)** helps accept new views, question existing values and energetically materialise spontaneous impulses **(B)** regulates muscle tension.
Bib.: [2]   Rarity: readily available ○

Iron Quartz
Mineralogy: crystal quartz containing iron (trig., primary/secondary)
Indications: **(SP)** energy **(S)** mobilises emotional and physical energy reserves; brings vigour **(M)** helps energetically pursue plans **(B)** improves performance; stimulates circulation and blood flow; fortifies blood vessels and muscles.
Bib.: [2]   Rarity: not always available ○

Jadeite (Jade)
Mineralogy: chain silicate of the pyroxene group (monocl., tert.)
Indications: **(SP)** balance **(S)** maintains balance between work and rest **(M)** aids childlike self-realisation **(B)** regulates the nerves, kidneys and adrenal glands (adrenaline production); maintains water, minerals and acid-base balance.
Bib.: [1] [2]   Rarity: not always available ○

Jadeite, black (Jade black)
Mineralogy: black jadeite (chain silicate, monoclinic, tertiary)
Indications: **(SP)** right measure **(S)** frees from negative emotions, calms and consolidates **(M)** helps remain neutral and find the right balance in one's activity **(B)** regulates elimination and excretion through the kidneys and bladder.
Bib.:   Rarity: scarce ○

Jamesonite Quartz
Mineralogy: jamesonite needles in quartz (monocl./trig., primary)
Indications: **(SP)** subordination **(S)** bestows discipline to overcome negative habits **(M)** helps place personal interests below higher ideals **(B)** helps with weak immunity as well as with problems of the bones, skin and nerves; enhances detoxification.
Bib.: [2]   Rarity: rare ○

Jasper, beige (Ivory Jasper)
Mineralogy: microcrystalline, grainy quartz (trigonal, secondary)
Indications: **(SP)** cleansing **(S)** brings constant, harmonious flow of power, helps avoid extremes **(M)** eases letting go of external thoughts **(B)** has a strong purifying effect; cleanses the connective tissues; alleviates allergies and skin problems.
Bib.: [2]   Rarity: readily available ○

Jasper, beige-brown (Cappuccino or Bruneau Jasper)
Mineralogy: microcrystalline, grainy quartz (trigonal, secondary)
Indications: **(SP)** performance **(S)** bestows stability, promotes inner calm **(M)** helps tackle a huge pile of work by sensibly apportioning one's energy **(B)** fortifies the stomach, intestine and immune system; promotes cleansing and elimination.
Bib.: [2]   Rarity: readily available ○

Jasper (Brecciated Jasper)
Mineralogy: breccia jasper with chalcedony sealing (trig., second.)
Indications: **(SP)** makes ready for conflicts **(S)** helps regain foothold over and over again after defeats **(M)** eases the resolving of conflicts and helps make up for damages **(B)** rejuvenates and vitalises; stimulates circulation, blood flow and self-healing power.
Bib.: [1] [2]   Rarity: common ○

Jasper, brown (Bat Cave Jasper)
Mineralogy: microcrystalline, grainy quartz (trigonal, secondary)
Indications: **(SP)** untiring **(S)** promotes stability, perseverance and flexibility (when necessary) **(M)** helps in the need for stamina in ongoing projects **(B)** stimulates digestion and elimination; stabilises circulation and helps with deep exhaustion.
Bib.: [2]   Rarity: readily available ○

Jasper, brownish-grey (Picture Jasper)

Mineralogy: microcrystalline, grainy quartz (trigonal, secondary)
Indications: (SP) helps come to terms with situations (S) helps bear energy-sapping situations in life (M) brings joy in simple things (B) enhances cleansing and purification of the connective tissues, stimulates elimination and alleviates allergic reactions.
Bib.: [2]   **Rarity:** readily available ○

Jasper, coloured (Rainbow Jasper)

Mineralogy: multicoloured jasper (quartz, trigonal, secondary)
Indications: (SP) creative power (S) rejuvenates and brings an active emotional life (M) supports creative realisation of one's ideas (B) enhances detoxification and the immune system; regenerates the functional tissue of organs (parenchyma).
Bib.: [1] [2]   **Rarity:** readily available ○

Jasper, green

Mineralogy: jasper containing iron silicate (quartz, trig., second.)
Indications: (SP) for resistance and harmony (S) calms emotions, helps express and accept them (M) improves control over thoughts and actions (B) fortifies the immune system, helps with 'flu, colds, infections and inflammation.
Bib.: [1] [2]   **Rarity:** readily available ○

Jasper with Hematite (Iron Jasper)

Mineralogy: mixture of jasper and hematite (oxide, trig., second.)
Indications: (SP) fitness (S) increases stamina under heavy strain (M) helps achieve and follow through one's ideas skilfully and emphatically (B) improves iron absorption and formation of red blood cells; stimulates circulation and blood flow.
Bib.: [1] [2]   **Rarity:** not always available ○

Jasper (Landscape Jasper, Kalahari Picture Stone)

Mineralogy: sandstone quartz (jasper, trigonal, secondary)
Indications: (SP) staying power (S) strengthens under long-lasting strain (M) helps tirelessly make new attempts after failures (B) aids digestion, the immune system and the cleansing of the connective tissues and so alleviates allergies and hay fever.
Bib.: [2]   **Rarity:** common ○

Jasper (Poppy Jasper)
Mineralogy: brightly patterned jasper (quartz, trigonal, secondary)
Indications: **(SP)** mood-enhancing **(S)** brings cheerfulness, gives impetus for variety and new experiences **(M)** stimulates imagination and versatility thus also helping to realise ideas **(B)** enhances the immune system, liver, circulation and regenerative powers.
Bib.: [1] [2]   **Rarity:** readily available ○

Jasper, red
Mineralogy: jasper containing hematite (quartz, trigonal, secondary)
Indications: **(SP)** willpower **(S)** makes courageous, dynamic; gives energy **(M)** gives courage for unpleasant tasks and makes spiritually alert **(B)** warms and enlivens; enhances blood flow, stimulates blood circulation and has a fever-enhancing effect (when necessary).
Bib.: [1] [2] [3]   **Rarity:** common ○

Jasper (Turitella Jasper)
Mineralogy: fossilised snail shells (jasper, trigonal, secondary)
Indications: **(SP)** withdrawal **(S)** helps overcome feelings of guilt **(M)** reminds of one's wishes, goals and plans **(B)** enhances detoxification and elimination; increases resistance against environmental pollution (dirt, toxin, radiation).
Bib.: [1] [2]   **Rarity:** common ○

Jasper (Vulcan Jasper)
Mineralogy: jasper containing chalcedony and hematite (trig., sec.)
Indications: **(SP)** alertness, caution **(S)** enhances one's sixth sense for dangers **(M)** helps act calmly, quickly and resolutely in critical situations **(B)** stimulates cleansing of the connective tissues, lymph and blood; activates the spleen, liver, kidneys and intestine.
Bib.: [1] [2]   **Rarity:** readily available ○

Jasper, yellow
Mineralogy: jasper containing limonite (quartz, trigonal, secondary)
Indications: **(SP)** endurance **(S)** promotes perseverance and tenacity **(M)** helps digest experiences and bear frustrating experiences **(B)** builds up a stable long-term immune protection; aids digestion; purifies and firms up the connective tissues.
Bib.: [1] [2]   **Rarity:** readily available ○

Jet (Gagate)

Mineralogy: carbon rock rich in bitumen (amorphous, secondary)
Indications: (SP) hope (S) helps overcome anxiety and depression (M) aids working on positive changes in a robust, unrelenting and persevering manner (B) helps with problems of the mouth, gum, intestine (diarrhoea), skin, joints and spine.
Bib.: [2] [3]   Rarity: readily available ○

Kimberlite

Mineralogy: volcano breccia (diverse structures, primary)
Indications: (SP) transformation (S) eases painful processes in life and gives new zeal (M) helps give up resistance against change and unites irreconcilables (B) promotes de-acidification and regulates the mineral balance in the body.
Bib.: [2]   Rarity: not always available ○

Kunzite (Spodumene)

Mineralogy: pink chain silicate (pyroxene group, monocl., prim.)
Indications: (SP) humility (S) improves empathy, helps with difficulties in making contact (M) helps accept criticism, promotes tolerance and readiness to serve (B) helps with neuralgia, sciatic neuralgia and toothache; releases tension in the heart region.
Bib.: [1] [2] [3]   Rarity: not always available ○

Labradorite (Feldspar)

Mineralogy: coloured glittering feldspar (lattice silicate, tricl., prim.)
Indications: (SP) reflection, truth (S) sharpens intuition, gives emotional depth and mediumistic abilities (M) brings forgotten memories to light and helps recognise illusions (B) reduces sensitivity to cold and blood pressure and alleviates rheumatism and gout.
Bib.: [1] [2]   Rarity: readily available ○

Labradorite (Feldspar, Spectrolite)

Mineralogy: very colourful labradorite (lattice silicate, tricl., prim.)
Indications: (SP) imagination, creativity (S) enhances artistic talents and a keen sense for harmonious connections (M) makes enthusiastic, imaginative and creative (B) reduces sensitivity to cold; alleviates rheumatism and gout.
Bib.: [1] [2]   Rarity: not always available ○

Labradorite, white (Feldspar, 'Rainbow Moonstone')
Mineralogy: blue shining white labradorite (triclinic, primary)
Indications: (SP) sensitivity (S) improves perceptive faculty, sleep and dream recall (M) promotes alertness and power of observation (B) improves sense of wellbeing; regulates the female hormonal cycle and helps with menstrual pains.
Bib.: [2]   **Rarity:** readily available ○

Lapis Lazuli
Mineralogy: lasurite rock (lasurite: lattice silicate, cubic, tertiary)
Indications: (SP) truth (S) promotes honesty, dignity, friendship and sociability (M) helps tell and accept the truth (B) helps with problems of the throat, larynx, vocal cords, nerves and brain; regulates the thyroid gland.
Bib.: [1] [2] [3]   **Rarity:** readily available ○

Lapis Lazuli with Calcite (Spotted Lapis)
Mineralogy: mixture of lapis lazuli and calcite (cubic/trigonal, tert.)
Indications: (SP) enhances sense of personal responsibility (S) promotes genuineness and helps gain control over one's life (M) enhances power of discernment and intelligence; helps open up to others (B) reduces fever and blood pressure; slows down the menstrual cycle.
Bib.: [1] [2] [3]   **Rarity:** readily available ○

Larimar (blue Pectolite)
Mineralogy: pectolite containing copper (chain silicate, tricl., prim.)
Indications: (SP) promotes openness (S) helps increase and demarcate spiritual space as well digest absorbed impressions (M) broadens sense of perception (B) stimulates brain activity and sensitivity; helps with problems of the chest, throat and head.
Bib.: [1] [2]   **Rarity:** not always available ○

Larvikite (Syenite)
Mineralogy: magmatite rich in feldspar (diverse structures, primary)
Indications: (SP) promotes clear assessment, straightforwardness (S) reduces emotions, makes sober and neutral (M) helps understand and resolve complicated facts (B) purifies the tissues, calms the nerves, cools and reduces blood pressure.
Bib.: [2]   **Rarity:** readily available ○

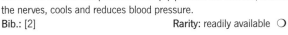

Lavender Jade (purple Jadeite)
Mineralogy: jadeite cont. manganese (chain silicate, monocl., tert.)
Indications: (SP) inner peace **(S)** brings inner harmony, eases nervousness and irritability **(M)** helps overcome disappointments and resolve conflicts in relationships **(B)** helps kidney problems; alleviates inflammation, pains in the heart and nerves; toothache.
Bib.: [1] [2] [3]   **Rarity:** scarce ○

Lavender Quartz (purple Chalcedony)
Mineralogy: lavender coloured chalcedony (trigonal, secondary)
Indications: (SP) understanding, sensitivity **(S)** combines calmness and attentiveness; makes sensitive to the needs of others **(M)** enhances understanding and readiness to continuously learn **(B)** fortifies the kidneys and secretion of the glands; reduces blood pressure.
Bib.: [2]   **Rarity:** not always available ○

Lazulite
Mineralogy: alkaline aluminium phosphate (monocl., prim./tert.)
Indications: (SP) spiritual orientation **(S)** makes emotions and feelings more obvious, bestows peace **(M)** aids reflection on meaning, value and importance of life **(B)** fortifies and relaxes; gently regulates the nerves, metabolism and hormone.
Bib.: [2]   **Rarity:** rare ○

Lemon Chrysoprase (Nickel Magnesite, Citron Chrysopr.)
Mineralogy: nickel magnesia chalcedony mixture (trig., second.)
Indications: (SP) life-affirming, frankness **(S)** cheers, helps overcome loneliness and inhibitions **(M)** makes self-critical, funny and clever **(B)** helpful for cleansing, with hyperacidity as well as stiff muscles and the effects of over-exertion.
Bib.: [2]   **Rarity:** scarce ○

Lepidolite
Mineralogy: lithium mica (sheet silicate, monoclinic, primary)
Indications: (SP) sets bounds **(S)** protects against external influences; gives inner peace; helps with sleep disorders **(M)** frees from distractions, helps concentrate on important aspects **(B)** alleviates pains in the joints and nerves, sciatica and neuralgia.
Bib.: [1] [2]   **Rarity:** readily available ○

Lime Oolite (Roe Stone, Margarita Stone)
Mineralogy: small spherical lime rocks (trig./orthorh., second.)
Indications: (SP) purification **(S)** brings relief in a gentle way, promotes night-long sleep **(M)** frees from nagging and 'brain racking' thoughts **(B)** reduces fever; detoxifies, cleanses and alleviates headaches originating from the metabolic system.
Bib.: [2]   **Rarity:** not always available ○

Limonite (Ironstone)
Mineralogy: limonite rock (iron oxide, orthorhombic, secondary)
Indications: (SP) promotes inner strength **(S)** gives strength under extreme strain; helps convert selfishness to a sense of community **(M)** helps remain firm in the face of attacks without fighting back **(B)** promotes cleansing; aids digestion and elimination.
Bib.: [2]   **Rarity:** readily available ○

Magnesite (nodule)
Mineralogy: magnesium carbonate (trigonal, secondary)
Indications: (SP) flexibility **(S)** helps become more flexible, without giving up one's plans; eases stress **(M)** promotes the ability to simply allow things to take their normal course instead of making a huge effort **(B)** detoxifies, de acidifies, eases strain and cramps.
Bib.: [1] [2] [3]   **Rarity:** readily available ○

Magnesite (rock)
Mineralogy: magnesium carbonate (trigonal, secondary)
Indications: (SP) relaxes **(S)** makes patient; helps with nervousness, timidness and irritability **(M)** promotes the art of listening **(B)** helps with migraine, headaches, cramps, colic and tension; guards against deposits in the vessels and heart attack.
Bib.: [1] [2] [3]   **Rarity:** common ○

Magnetite
Mineralogy: magnetic iron oxide (cubic, primary/tertiary)
Indications: (SP) for activation and orientation **(S)** increases reflex action **(M)** stimulates aligning oneself with higher ideals; helps differentiate between useful and useless things **(B)** stimulates energy flow and activities of the glands; activates the liver and bile production.
Bib.: [2]   **Rarity:** readily available ○

Magnetite Jade (Nephrite with Magnetite)
Mineralogy: mixture of magnetite and nephrite (cubic/monocl., tert.)
Indications: (SP) addresses inner attitude (S) helps change negative behavioural patterns, promotes a constructive attitude to life (M) encourages reflection on thoughts, actions and their resulting effects (B) stimulates brain, nerves, hormonal glands, liver, kidneys.
Bib.: [2]   **Rarity:** not always available ○

Malachite
Mineralogy: alkaline copper carbonate (monoclinic, secondary)
Indications: (SP) promotes adventurous intensive life (S) deepens emotional life, helps with sexual difficulties (M) promotes power of imagination and decision (B) stimulates the brain, nerves and liver, detoxifies and helps with rheumatism, cramps and menstrual pains.
Bib.: [1] [2] [3]   **Rarity:** readily available ○

Marble
Mineralogy: metamorphic lime (calcium carbonate, trigonal, tertiary)
Indications: (SP) aids transformation (S) changes inner discontentment and unhappy life circumstances (M) opens up new perspectives, brings creative solutions to problems (B) enhances the development of children; fortifies the kidneys and spleen; alleviates allergies.
Bib.: [1] [2]   **Rarity:** readily available ○

Marble (Zebra Marble)
Mineralogy: marble with manganese (calcium carbonate, trig., tert.)
Indications: (SP) self-liberation (S) helps defend oneself against suppression, improves discontentment (M) helps overcome resignation (B) promotes cleansing and elimination; eases allergies; fortifies the spleen, kidneys, intestine, tissues and skin.
Bib.: [1] [2]   **Rarity:** readily available ○

Marcasite
Mineralogy: iron sulphide (orthorhombic, primary/secondary)
Indications: (SP) addresses self-worth (S) helps appreciate oneself and brings suppressed desires to light (M) helps recognition of the causes of one's unhappiness and to give up adaptations and subservient behaviours (B) stimulates detoxification and elimination.
Bib.: [2]   **Rarity:** not always available ○

Moldavite

Mineralogy: glass formed by meteorite impact (amorphous)

Indications: (SP) freedom (S) brings unlimited expanse; promotes dreams and memories (M) removes attention from strong vices; promotes the recognition of one being of spiritual origin (B) helps with diseases of the respiratory tract, 'flu and anaemia.

Bib.: [1] [2]   **Rarity:** not always available ○

Mondolite (Iron Quartz-Chalcedony)

Mineralogy: iron quartz on chalcedony (quartz, trigonal, secondary)

Indications: (SP) alertness (S) strengthens and harmonises; invigorates and dispels tiredness (M) makes alert and endows quick reflexes (B) stimulates digestion, blood flow and the immune system; helps with interruption and delay of menstruation.

Bib.: –   **Rarity:** scarce ○

Mookaite

Mineralogy: mixture of jasper and opalite (trig./amorph., second.)

Indications: (SP) experience (S) promotes variety, fun and intense experiences (M) makes flexible, prompts one to envisage many possibilities and to choose suitable one (B) fortifies the spleen, liver, immune system, enhances blood purification and wound healing.

Bib.: [1] [2] [3]   **Rarity:** readily available ○

Moonstone (Feldspar)

Mineralogy: feldspar with swaying light beam (monoclinic, prim.)

Indications: (SP) intuition (S) bestows depth of feeling, helps with sleepwalking (M) makes receptive to inspiration and impulses (B) brings hormonal cycles in harmony with natural rhythms, helps with problems during menstruation, menopause and after childbirth.

Bib.: [1] [2] [3]   **Rarity:** readily available ○

Moqui Marbles (Limonite Balls)

Mineralogy: limonite balls filled with sand (trig./orthorh., second.)

Indications: (SP) fulfilment of wishes (S) motivates during daytime and increases desire for sleep at night (M) brings wishes and needs closer (B) promotes regeneration, blood formation and blood flow; revives from latent illnesses; fortifies the muscles, intestine and skin.

Bib.: [2]   **Rarity:** rare ○

Morganite

Mineralogy: beryl cont. manganese (ring silicate, hexagonal, prim.)
Indications: (SP) responsibility **(S)** helps do away with stress, pressure to perform, pomposity and habit of fleeing **(M)** makes considerate, helps take on responsibility **(B)** ameliorates problems of the heart and nerves, sense of balance disorders and impotence.
Bib.: [1] [2]   **Rarity:** scarce ○

Moss Agate

Mineralogy: chalcedony with green dendrites (trigonal, secondary)
Indications: (SP) liberation **(S)** frees from heaviness, pressure and strain **(M)** makes conscious, promotes communication and an alert mind **(B)** cleanses the tissues, lymph and respiratory tract; helps with cough, colds and stubborn infections and reduces fever.
Bib.: [1] [2] [3]   **Rarity:** readily available ○

Moss Agate, pink

Mineralogy: chalcedony with brown chlorite (trigonal, secondary)
Indications: (SP) coming to terms **(S)** helps overcome revulsion, disgust, resentment and an aggressive nature **(M)** helps give up apportioning of blame and thoughts of revenge **(B)** stimulates digestion and excretion; improves activities of the intestine and intestinal flora.
Bib.: [2] [3]   **Rarity:** not always available ○

Muscovite

Mineralogy: light mica (sheet silicate, monoclinic, primary/tertiary)
Indications: (SP) protection **(S)** helps remain relaxed and calm in the face of serious problems, provocations and attacks **(M)** helps see things clearly and still remain objective **(B)** helps with problems of stomach, gallbladder, kidneys; trembling and nervousness.
Bib.: [2]   **Rarity:** readily available ○

Natrolite

Mineralogy: zeolite fibre (lattice silicate, orthorhombic, primary/tert.)
Indications: (SP) wholeness, identity **(S)** helps trust one's inner voice **(M)** promotes an all-embracing way of perceiving and viewing things **(B)** regulates the kidneys, thyroid gland and hormone system, fortifies the intestine, connective tissues, muscles and skin.
Bib.: [2]   **Rarity:** scarce ○

Nephrite

Mineralogy: interwoven actinolite (chain silicate, monoclinic, tert.)
Indications: **(SP)** balance **(S)** protection against external pressure and aggressiveness; brings inner balance **(M)** helps with indecision, doubt and senseless brooding **(B)** fortifies the kidneys, regulates water balance, and helps with problems of the urinary tract and bladder.
Bib.: [1] [2] [3]   **Rarity:** readily available ○

Nickel Quartz

Mineralogy: coarse quartz containing nickel (trigonal, primary)
Indications: **(SP)** revelation, confession **(S)** makes it easier to express discord, anger and displeasure **(M)** helps resolve misunderstandings and admit mistakes **(B)** enhances detoxification, helps with dizziness and balance-related disorders.
Bib.: –   **Rarity:** scarce ○

Nickeline (Red Nickel Pyrite)

Mineralogy: nickel arsenide (trigonal, secondary)
Indications: **(SP)** moderation and circumspection **(S)** helps with excessive self-destructive lifestyle **(M)** improves consideration for others **(B)** helps with nodes in the tissues, and rashes.
Caution: very poisonous! Avoid skin contact and internal usage!
Bib.: –   **Rarity:** scarce ○

Nuumite

Mineralogy: anthophyllite rock (chain silicate, orthorhombic, tertiary)
Indications: **(SP)** honour, respect **(S)** reduces tension and stress, aids deep sleep **(M)** helps respect oneself and others and fulfil duties agreed on **(B)** helps with diseases of the nerves as well as with problems of the kidneys, and ears.
Bib.: [4]   **Rarity:** rare ○

Obsidian

Mineralogy: volcanic glass (silicon dioxide, amorphous, primary)
Indications: **(SP)** resolution **(S)** rescue remedy for shock, traumas and blockages **(M)** helps integrate one's dark side, activates untapped abilities **(B)** eases pain, tension and constriction of the vessels and enhances blood flow and wound healing.
Bib.: [1] [2] [3]   **Rarity:** common ○

Obsidian (Gold Sheen Obsidian)

Mineralogy: gold iridescent volcanic glass (amorphous, primary)
Indications: (SP) healing **(S)** helps overcome effects of emotional injuries **(M)** helps dispel deep-rooted pessimism **(B)** accelerates healing of injuries, wounds, distortions, bruises and sprains.
Bib.: [2]   Rarity: scarce ○

Obsidian (Mahogany Obsidian)

Mineralogy: brownish black volcanic glass (amorphous, primary)
Indications: (SP) drive **(S)** brings power, initiative and new drive **(M)** dispels dismay caused by insults, disparaging comments and false accusations **(B)** improves blood flow; warms up the limbs; helps stop bleeding and aids wound healing.
Bib.: [1] [2]   Rarity: readily available ○

Obsidian (Rainbow Obsidian)

Mineralogy: coloured iridescent volcanic glass (amorphous, prim.)
Indications: (SP) clairvoyance **(S)** lends the world of perceptions an undreamed-of depth, protects and strengthens at the same time **(M)** makes open; intensifies perception and sharpens the receptive senses **(B)** improves blood flow, eases pain and helps with bad eyesight.
Bib.: [1] [2] [3]   Rarity: rare ○

Obsidian (Silver Sheen Obsidian)

Mineralogy: silver iridescent volcanic glass (amorphous, primary)
Indications: (SP) consciousness **(S)** reveals suppressed thoughts and emotions; helps ward off psychic attacks **(M)** improves sense of perception, sharpens senses and intellect **(B)** releases shock on the cellular level and brings stagnant healing processes into motion.
Bib.: [1] [2]   Rarity: scarce ○

Obsidian (Smoky Obsidian, Apache Tear)

Mineralogy: transparent volcanic glass (amorphous, primary)
Indications: (SP) eases pain **(S)** releases emotional pain and helps with fear, panic and shock **(M)** helps give up belief in misfortune **(B)** alleviates sprain, strain, back pain as well as general local and inter-mittent pains.
Bib.: [1] [2] [3]   Rarity: readily available ○

Obsidian (Snowflake Obsidian)

Mineralogy: obsidian with feldspar (amorphous/triclinic, primary)

Indications: (SP) awakening **(S)** dispels fear and emotional blockages **(M)** motivates to spontaneously materialise ideas **(B)** enhances blood flow even under extreme under-supply ('smoker's leg'), warms up the hands and feet, aids wound healing.

Bib.: [1] [2] [3]   Rarity: common ○

Ocean Jasper (Ocean Agate, Orbicular Jasper)

Mineralogy: spherulitic chalcedony (quartz, trigonal, primary)

Indications: (SP) renewal **(S)** makes positive, able to withstand stress; helps with relaxing sleep **(M)** helps resolve conflicts **(B)** aids digestion, warmth, detoxification, regeneration, cell renewal, the immune system and skin; helps with colds, cysts and tumours.

Bib.: [4]   Rarity: not always available ○

Olivine, Spanish (Peridotite, Dunite)

Mineralogy: fine crystalline peridotite (island silicate, orthorh., prim.)

Indications: (SP) independence, protection **(S)** brings balance and the feeling of being protected **(M)** improves concentration and aids self-determination **(B)** regulates metabolism and the harmonious working together of the internal organs; helps isolate foreign bodies.

Bib.: –   Rarity: rare ○

Onyx

Mineralogy: black chalcedony (trigonal, primary/secondary)

Indications: (SP) self-assertion **(S)** boosts self-confidence and sense of responsibility **(M)** improves rational thinking, logic, control and power of reasoning **(B)** sharpens sense of hearing, helps with diseases of the inner ear; improves functions of the nerves.

Bib.: [1] [2]   Rarity: not always available ○

Onyx Marble (Aragonite Calcite)

Mineralogy: banded aragonite calcite (orthorhombic, secondary)

Indications: (SP) rhythmic development; relief **(S)** makes more relaxed, freer and more sensitive **(M)** makes flexible; brings rest and activity into a harmonious balance **(B)** helps with problems of the liver, gallbladder, discs, joints and meniscus.

Bib.: [2]   Rarity: common ○

Oolite (Iron Oolite)
Mineralogy: small iron oxide balls in sandstone (div. str., second.)
Indications: (SP) health consciousness **(S)** curbs consuming workaholism and enhances regeneration **(M)** turns attention to health and fitness **(B)** promotes blood flow and supply of nutrients to the tissues; fortifies the nerves, muscles, intestine and skin.
Bib.: [2]   **Rarity:** not always available ○

Opal, blue
Mineralogy: blue opal (silicon dioxide, amorphous, secondary)
Indications: (SP) sixth sense **(S)** promotes empathy **(M)** improves communication, helps understand others and express oneself clearly **(B)** reduces blood pressure and fever, stimulates water balance, lymph and the kidneys.
Bib.: [2]   **Rarity:** not always available ○

Opal, Cat's Eye
Mineralogy: opal with glimmer of light (amorphous, secondary)
Indications: (SP) helps comprehend **(S)** cheers up when despondent, brings hope and optimism **(M)** allows new views while emphasising the positive aspects **(B)** stimulates the nerves, brain and sensory organs; improves sense of touch.
Bib.: [2]   **Rarity:** rare ○

Opal (Chrysopal, Andean Opal)
Mineralogy: opal cont. copper (silicon dioxide, amorphous, second.)
Indications: (SP) naturalness **(S)** releases emotions, relieves feeling of unease; lightens mood **(M)** helps look at the world with amazement and to recognise the miracle of life **(B)** detoxifies; reduces fever; fortifies the liver and kidneys.
Bib.: [1] [2]   **Rarity:** not always available ○

Opal, colourless (Andean Opal)
Mineralogy: colourless opal (silicon dioxide, amorphous, secondary)
Indications: (SP) motion in life **(S)** makes flexible and helps adjust to changing situations **(M)** brings thoughts, speech and deeds into motion **(B)** enhances purification of the skin and respiratory tract, stimulates flow of the lymph and excretion.
Bib.: [1] [2]   **Rarity:** not always available ○

Opal (Dendritic Opal)

Mineralogy: opal with manganese dendrites (amorphous, pr./sec.)
Indications: (SP) contact (S) helps remain open and approachable in spite of bad experiences (M) improves contact with the environment and fellow human beings (B) cleanses, enhances lymph flow and excretion; helps with colds and effects of smoking.
Bib.: [2]   **Rarity:** not always available ○

Opal, green

Mineralogy: mixture of opal and nontronite (amorph/monoc., prim.)
Indications: (SP) life perspectives (S) brings quick recovery from exhaustion (M) helps with disorientation and turns attention to fulfilling aspects of life (B) promotes regeneration; fortifies the liver, kidneys and gonads (ovary, testicle).
Bib.: [1] [2]   **Rarity:** scarce ○

Opal (Hyalite, Water Opal)

Mineralogy: crystal-clear opal without colour play (amorph., prim.)
Indications: (SP) instinct (S) brings clarity in emotions, helps be in the right place at the right time (M) helps recognise and express inner needs (B) enhances water balance and fortifies the eyes, ears, sense of smell and taste.
Bib.: [2]   **Rarity:** rare ○

Opal in Matrix (Leopard Opal)

Mineralogy: small precious opal bubbles in basalt rock (amorp., pr.)
Indications: (SP) enjoyment (S) intensifies all experiences, deepens emotions and brings comfort during fear or grief (M) aids living in the present (B) enhances growth, supply of nutrients and regulation of metabolism in the cells and tissues.
Bib.: [2]   **Rarity:** scarce ○

Opal (Moss Opal)

Mineralogy: opal with diverse inclusions (amorphous, prim./secon.)
Indications: (SP) participation (S) helps one better enter relationships or groups (M) helps approach others without prejudice (B) cleanses the lymph, respiratory tract; helps with coughs and colds; enhances cleansing, digestion and excretion.
Bib.: [2]   **Rarity:** not always available ○

Opal (Pink Opal, Andean Opal)
Mineralogy: opal cont. manganese (silicon dioxide, amorph, secon.)
Indications: (SP) warmth (S) dissipates awkwardness, shame and shyness; enhances perceptive ability and affection (M) makes friendly and open in thoughts and actions (B) helps with heart problems, especially those caused by worrying about the heart.
Bib.: [1] [2]   **Rarity:** not always available ○

Opal (Prase Opal)
Mineralogy: opal cont. nickel (silicon dioxide, amorphous, second.)
Indications: (SP) casualness (S) frees from fear, insecurity and feeling of guilt (M) helps unburden one's heart (B) enhances the detoxification and cleansing of the body fluids; strengthens the liver and kidneys and helps with rheumatism and gout.
Bib.: [2]   **Rarity:** scarce ○

Opal, Precious Opal (Boulder Opal)
Mineralogy: opal veins in bedrock (opal: amorphous, secondary)
Indications: (SP) humour (S) makes extravert and helps infect others with one's joy (M) helps survive adverse situations with optimism (B) stimulates the lymph, kidneys and intestine and the supply of nutrients to the cells.
Bib.: [1] [2] [3]   **Rarity:** not always available ○

Opal, Precious Opal (Crystal Opal)
Mineralogy: clear, very colourful precious opal (amorph., second.)
Indications: (SP) high spirits (S) brings joy, exuberance and a deep feeling of joy (M) inspires imagination, art and poetry, makes clever and creative (B) improves the auto-regulation of the whole organism, keeps healthy and supports all healing processes.
Bib.: [2] [3]   **Rarity:** rare ○

Opal, Precious Opal (Yowah Nut)
Mineralogy: filigree boulder opal (opal: amorphous, secondary)
Indications: (SP) life-dream (S) promotes a loving feeling for one's body and earthly existence; stimulates day and night dreaming (M) increases power of imagination (B) enhances the immune system and self-healing power, helps with very severe illnesses.
Bib.: [1] [2] [3]   **Rarity:** not always available ○

Opal, Precious Opal, black (Black Opal)

Mineralogy: black colourful precious opal (amorphous, secondary)
Indications: (SP) will to live **(S)** aids a positive disposition to life; helps with anxiety and depression **(M)** helps easily accept difficulties **(B)** stimulates intensive cleansing processes, enhances cleansing and excretion; has a regenerative effect after illnesses.
Bib.: [1] [2] [3]   **Rarity:** rare ○

Opal, Precious Opal, white (Light Opal)

Mineralogy: light colourful precious opal (amorphous, secondary)
Indications: (SP) joie de vivre **(S)** helps enjoy the beautiful side of life, boosts sensuality and eroticism **(M)** awakens enthusiasm, imagination and creativity **(B)** mobilises the lymph, cleanses and helps with coughs and diseases of the respiratory tract.
Bib.: [1] [2] [3]   **Rarity:** not always available ○

Opal, white (Milk Opal)

Mineralogy: white opal (silicon oxide, amorphous, primary/second.)
Indications: (SP) open-mindedness **(S)** makes open and accommodating; helps accept oneself and others **(M)** aids communication, exchange and companionship **(B)** stimulates lymph flow, the kidneys, bladder and the regulation of water balance.
Bib.: [2]   **Rarity:** not always available ○

Opalite

Mineralogy: rock containing opal (opal: amorphous, secondary)
Indications: (SP) sociability **(S)** helps dissipate fear of physical contact and integrate oneself in communities **(M)** for a good contact with the environment **(B)** enhances cleansing, detoxification and excretion; purifies the connective tissues, intestine and mucous membranes.
Bib.: [2]   **Rarity:** not always available ○

Ophicalcite (Connemara, Verd Antique)

Mineralogy: silicate marble with calcite, serpentine, talc etc. (tert.)
Indications: (SP) refreshment, comfort **(S)** helps become optimistic in unpleasant circumstances as well as to overcome grief and resignation **(M)** helps think calmly and constructively **(B)** helps with problems of the heart, kidneys, large intestine, liver and gallbladder.
Bib.: [2]   **Rarity:** scarce ○

Orthoclase (Feldspar, Goldorthoclase)
Mineralogy: potassium feldspar (lattice silicate, monoclinic, primary)
Indications: (SP) perception (S) makes optimistic, buoyant and elated (M) dissipates anxiety, doubt and distrust; refines the perceptive faculty (B) helps with problems of the stomach, heart, constriction of the chest, restlessness and insomnia.
Bib.: [2]   **Rarity:** not always available ○

Pallasite
Mineralogy: iron meteorite with olivine (cubic/orthor., interplanetary)
Indications: (SP) insight into the origins of everything (S) frees from addiction and binding commitments (M) urges to discover one's inner world (B) detoxifies and fortifies the liver, gallbladder, intestine and muscles.
Bib.: [2]   **Rarity:** rare ○

Peridote (Olivine, Chrysolite)
Mineralogy: magnesium iron island silicate (orthorhombic, primary)
Indications: (SP) independence (S) dissipates anger, rage and guilty conscience (M) helps break away from external influences as well as to admit mistakes (B) strengthens the liver, gallbladder and small intestine; detoxifies and helps with infections, fungi and warts.
Bib.: [1] [2] [3]   **Rarity:** readily available ○

Petalite
Mineralogy: lithium aluminium sheet silicate (monoclinic, primary)
Indications: (SP) self-recognition, search for identity (S) helps loosen up hardened feelings and face difficulties rather than fleeing (M) makes honest and helps come to terms with painful recognitions (B) alleviates severe pains and helps with diseases of the heart, nerves and eyes.
Bib.: [2]   **Rarity:** scarce ○

Petrified Palm Wood
Mineralogy: palm wood transformed into quartz (trigonal, second.)
Indications: (SP) composure (S) makes emotions flow better and leads them back to a point of calm (M) gives presence of mind and a quick reaction (B) regulates fluid and metabolism in the whole body.
Bib.: [1] [2] [3]   **Rarity:** not always available ○

Petrified Wood (opalised)
Mineralogy: Fossilised wood transformed into opal (amorph., secon.)
Indications: (SP) life-affirming **(S)** makes open and lively with an unshakeable inner harmony **(M)** helps see the pleasant, positive side of life **(B)** gives a healthy appetite, aids digestion, cleansing and excretion.
Bib.: [1] [2] [3]   **Rarity:** not always available ○

Petrified Wood (Peanut Wood)
Mineralogy: fossilised wood with worm passages (trig., secondary)
Indications: (SP) contentment **(S)** brings wellbeing and makes it easier to accept life the way it is **(M)** helps use approaching external changes for one's own objectives **(B)** calms the nerves, helps with overweight caused by 'inadequate earthing'.
Bib.: [1] [2] [3]   **Rarity:** not always available ○

Petrified Wood (silicified)
Mineralogy: Fossilised wood transformed into quartz (trig., second.)
Indications: (SP) well rooted **(S)** makes stable and firmly 'rooted' in oneself **(M)** helps 'stand with both feet on the firm ground of reality' **(B)** stimulates digestion and metabolism, fortifies the nerves and helps with overweight caused by 'inadequate earthing'.
Bib.: [1] [2] [3]   **Rarity:** readily available ○

Phlogopite
Mineralogy: magnesium mica (sheet silicate, monoclinic, tertiary)
Indications: (SP) devotion, modesty, protection **(S)** helps retain innocence and trust **(M)** reduces excessively high demands **(B)** eases travelling sickness and discomforts caused by inner tension; relaxes the muscles and aids birth.
Bib.: [2] – see 'Hermanov Balls'   **Rarity:** scarce ○

Picasso Marble (Limestone)
Mineralogy: lime rock (calcium carbonate, trigonal, secondary)
Indications: (SP) abstraction, extracting the essence **(S)** helps remain faithful to oneself **(M)** helps recognise the essentials and perseveringly turn ideas into deeds **(B)** enhances calcium metabolism, strengthens the large intestine, connective tissues and bones.
Bib.: [2] [13]   **Rarity:** readily available ○

Piemontite Quartz Mica

Mineralogy: manganese-epidote in rock (monocl./trig., tert.)
Indications: (SP) courage, confidence **(S)** helps approach others, deal with embarrassing experiences; lends creative sexuality **(M)** helps express one's needs **(B)** supports the heart, liver, regeneration and fertility, strengthens the sexual organs.
Bib.: [2]   **Rarity:** readily available ○

Pietersite

Mineralogy: tiger's eye and falcon's eye breccia (trig., second.)
Indications: (SP) change **(S)** helps in turbulent times; dissipates unpleasant feelings **(M)** helps digest impressions faster and overcome conflicts **(B)** eases headaches, nervous diseases, difficulties in breathing, stomach pain and dizziness.
Bib.: [1] [2]   **Rarity:** not always available ○

Pink Quartz

Mineralogy: pink crystalline quartz (silicon dioxide, trigonal, primary)
Indications: (SP) self-development **(S)** makes lively and cheerful, brings joie de vivre; enhances personal talents **(M)** helps the unfolding of things one enjoys doing and creates soothing ambience **(B)** brings wellbeing, soothes the nerves and overwrought senses.
Bib.: [2]   **Rarity:** rare ○

Plasma

Mineralogy: green chalcedony (quartz, trigonal, primary/secondary)
Indications: (SP) for calm **(S)** helps with irritability and aggression; increases staying power **(M)** has a harmonising effect on flighty, disorganised thoughts and actions **(B)** boosts immune reaction and regenerative power; alleviates inflammations.
Bib.: [2]   **Rarity:** scarce ○

Pop-Rocks (Boji's, Pyrite Balls)

Mineralogy: pyrite nodules in limonite coating (cubic/orthorh., sec.)
Indications: (SP) energy flow **(S)** intensifies emotions and moods **(M)** helps recognise inhibiting patterns **(B)** good for preventive health care; painlessly dissipates mild blockages and makes conscious of more severe ones, promotes cleansing and excretion.
Bib.: [1] [2]   **Rarity:** rare ○

Porcellanite (Eye Porcellanite)

Mineralogy: metamorphic clay (sheet silicate, monocl./triclinic, tert.)
Indications: **(SP)** ability to differentiate **(S)** helps better perceive emotions **(M)** improves the ability to distinguish between meaning, value and importance **(B)** helps with acne, allergic skin rashes, hyperacidity and chronic tiredness.
Bib.: [2]   **Rarity:** scarce ○

Porcellanite (Landscape Porcellanite)

Mineralogy: metamorphic clay (sheet silicate, monocl./triclinic, tert.)
Indications: **(SP)** ability to perform **(S)** helps express feelings **(M)** promotes creativity and ability to perform **(B)** helps with hyperacidity; cleanses the connective tissues, skin, intestine and respiratory tract, enhances excretion and invigorates in cases of chronic fatigue.
Bib.: [2]   **Rarity:** scarce ○

Porphyrite (Chrysanthemenstone)

Mineralogy: feldspar in andesite matrix (feldspar: triclinic, primary)
Indications: **(SP)** circumspection **(S)** brings calm and sensible activity; helps with restlessness caused by stimulus satiation **(M)** helps wait for and grab the right opportunity to materialise ideas and projects **(B)** calms and strengthens the nerves and senses.
Bib.: [1] [2]   **Rarity:** not always available ○

Porphyrite (Flower Porphyry)

Mineralogy: feldspar in andesite matrix (feldspar: triclinic, primary)
Indications: **(SP)** circumspection **(S)** makes patient and strong at new beginnings **(M)** allows ideas to mature before being put into action; encourages sensible caution **(B)** calms and strengthens the nerves, enhances the senses and keeps the muscles flexible.
Bib.: [1] [2]   **Rarity:** not always available ○

Prase

Mineralogy: crystal quartz with silicate inclusions (trigonal, primary)
Indications: **(SP)** gentleness **(S)** calms overwrought nerves and makes it easier to resolve conflicts **(M)** helps people who bear grudges let go of the past **(B)** eases pain, reduces fever and heals swellings and bruises; helps with problems of the bladder.
Bib.: [1] [2] [3]   **Rarity:** scarce ○

Prase Quartz (Buddstone)

Mineralogy: coarse quartz with silicate inclusions (trigonal, tertiary)
Indications: (SP) self-control (S) makes it easier to give up rage and fury (M) helps to retain self-control under emotional onslaughts (B) alleviates effects of radiation, sunburn, sunstroke, heatstroke and insect bites; helps with problems of the bladder.
Bib.: [1] [2] [3]   **Rarity:** not always available ○

Prasiolite Amethyst (Amegreen, Sambesite)

Mineralogy: violet-green crystal quartz (quartz, trigonal, primary)
Indications: (SP) authenticity, self-assertion (S) helps stand by one's feelings (M) prompts to defend one's conviction in a determined way (B) regulates breath, the heart and circulation; good for the hair and nails; releases tension and aids excretion.
Bib.: [2]   **Rarity:** rare ○

Prehnite, green

Mineralogy: calcium aluminium group silicate (orthorhombic, prim.)
Indications: (SP) acceptance (S) makes it easier to accept oneself and others (M) helps accept unpleasant truths and enhances receptive ability (B) aids detoxification/processing of fat-soluble substances, stimulates fat metabolism and renewal processes.
Bib.: [1] [2]   **Rarity:** not always available ○

Prehnite, yellow

Mineralogy: calcium aluminium group silicate (orthorhombic, prim.)
Indications: (SP) respect (S) promotes respect for others; helps command acknowledgement (M) dissipates repressive and evasive mechanisms (B) aids detoxification/processing of fat-soluble substances; stimulates fat metabolism and helps with excess weight.
Bib.: [1] [2]   **Rarity:** not always available ○

Printstone (Sandstone)

Mineralogy: sandstone quartz with iron oxides (trigonal, secondary)
Indications: (SP) feeling of wellbeing (S) helps restful sleep; invigorates and endows with a deep sense of 'holiday' (M) improves body awareness (B) gently enhances breathing, circulation, digestion and excretion.
Bib.: [2]   **Rarity:** not always available ○

Psilomelane (Brownstone)

Mineralogy: manganese oxide (orthorhombic, primary/secondary)
Indications: (SP) promotes slowness (S) helps come to terms with negative experiences (M) slows down hasty processes, helps to save energy (B) strengthens when under energy-sapping strain; stimulates the intestine, stabilises circulation and protects the heart.
Bib.: [2] **Rarity:** not always available ○

Purpurite

Mineralogy: manganese iron phosphate (orthorhombic, primary)
Indications: (SP) inspiration (S) helps with tiredness, exhaustion and despondency (M) improves alertness, awareness and receptive ability (B) gives energy; helps with cardiac insufficiency and functional disorders of the sensory organs.
Bib.: [2] **Rarity:** scarce ○

Pyrite (Cluster)

Mineralogy: brass-coloured iron sulphide (cubic, prim./secondary)
Indications: (SP) self-recognition (S) exposes secrets and suppressed memories (M) makes open, direct and honest; reveals the causes of certain circumstances and illnesses (B) stimulates the liver, intestine, detoxification and excretion.
Bib.: [1] [2] **Rarity:** readily available ○

Pyrite (Cubes)

Mineralogy: cube-shaped iron sulphide (cubic, secondary)
Indications: (SP) ability to mirror (S) urges perseverance in search for solutions during conflicts (M) promotes the insight that things that disturb us in others are also present in us (B) clarifies confusing presentations of diseases and brings out the causal symptom.
Bib.: [1] [2] **Rarity:** readily available ○

Pyrite (Sun)

Mineralogy: radial iron sulphide (cubic, tertiary)
Indications: (SP) resolution (S) helps laugh at oneself (M) frees from thoughts fixed on misfortune, misery and anguish (B) alleviates pains like back pain and problem of the joints etc. and releases cramps and menstrual pains.
Bib.: [1] [2] [3] **Rarity:** rare ○

Pyrite Agate

Mineralogy: mixture of chalcedony and pyrite (trig./cubic, second.)
Indications: (SP) purification **(S)** helps overcome heaviness and strain **(M)** prompts to tackle unpleasant situations **(B)** promotes purification and lymph flow, stimulates the liver, improves elimination and accelerates healing processes.
Bib.: [2]   **Rarity:** not always available ○

Pyrophyllite

Mineralogy: alkaline aluminium sheet silicate (monoclinic, primary)
Indications: (SP) self-determination **(S)** helps set boundaries and to remain alert in confusing situations **(M)** helps detach oneself from externally imposed obligations **(B)** helps with hyperacidity, stomach pains and heartburns.
Bib.: –   **Rarity:** scarce ○

Smoky Quartz

Mineralogy: brown crystal quartz (trigonal, primary)
Indications: (SP) relaxation **(S)** releases tension and helps with stress **(M)** enhances rational, realistic and pragmatic thought processes **(B)** helps with headaches, tense shoulders and back, relieves pains and strengthens the nerves.
Bib.: [1] [2] [3]   **Rarity:** readily available ○

Smoky Quartz, dark (Morion)

Mineralogy: dark to black crystal quartz (trigonal, primary)
Indications: (SP) withstanding exertion **(S)** helps better cope with strain and stress **(M)** makes alert and industrious, helps tackle important things with zeal **(B)** relieves pain and helps with frequent exposure to radiations (e.g. X-rays).
Bib.: [1] [2]   **Rarity:** scarce ○

Smoky Quartz with Phantom

Mineralogy: smoky quartz with obvious markings of growth stages
Indications: (SP) willpower **(S)** dissipates fear of failure, defeat or pain **(M)** helps master difficult, depressing situations and mature in the process **(B)** strengthens the senses and nerves, helps with pain and tense muscles.
Bib.: [1] [2] – see 'Phantom Quartz'   **Rarity:** scarce ○

Strawberry Quartz

Mineralogy: manganese pink coloured quartz (trigonal, primary)
Indications: (SP) shows cause and effect **(S)** helps not to attach too much importance to oneself; makes witty and humorous **(M)** shows how one personally gives rise to misfortune and failure **(B)** helps with agitation, constriction, and disorders of the heart and circulation.
Bib.: [2]   **Rarity:** readily available ○

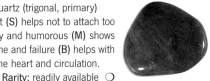

Rhodochrosite

Mineralogy: pink to red manganese carbonate (trigonal, secondary)
Indications: (SP) activity **(S)** makes buoyant and cheerful, enhances sexuality and eroticism **(M)** makes dynamic, active and makes things work faster **(B)** boosts circulation, increases blood pressure and helps with abdominal pains and migraine.
Bib.: [1] [2] [3]   **Rarity:** not always available ○

Rhodonite

Mineralogy: calcium manganese chain silicate (triclinic, tertiary)
Indications: (SP) wound healing **(S)** helps forgiveness **(M)** promotes mutual understanding **(B)** best stone for injuries, bleeding wounds and insect bites; strengthens muscles, heart and circulation; helps with autoimmune diseases and stomach ulcers.
Bib.: [1] [2] [3]   **Rarity:** readily available ○

Rhyolite (Eye Jasper, Rain Forest Jasper)

Mineralogy: vulcanite rich in silicic acid (diverse structures, primary)
Indications: (SP) intensification **(S)** consolidates existing circumstances; helps accept oneself as one is **(M)** helps see/assess one's situation more clearly **(B)** alleviates 'flu, colds and infections.
Bib.: [1] [2]   **Rarity:** readily available ○

Rhyolite (Dr. Liesegang Stone, Aztec Stone)

Mineralogy: vulcanite rich in silicic acid (diverse structures, primary)
Indications: (SP) fortification **(S)** consolidates existing circumstances; promotes self-esteem **(M)** helps master hard situations calmly and resolutely **(B)** enhances resistance and the immune system; stimulates the small and large intestines.
Bib.: [2]   **Rarity:** not always available ○

Rhyolite (Leopard Skin Jasper)
Mineralogy: vulcanite rich in silicic acid (diverse structures, primary)
Indications: (SP) consolidation (S) for balance between activity and rest/good deep sleep (M) allows clear focus on what needs to be done (B) stimulates digestion and excretion; helps with skin problems and hardened tissues.
Bib.: [1] [2]   Rarity: common ○

Richterite
Mineralogy: chain silicate rich in mineral elements (monoclinic, tert.)
Indications: (SP) wisdom, foresight (S) gives a good sense of right timing (M) broadens one's horizons; helps recognise trends early and assess them (B) enhances the kidneys and regulates mineral balance.
Bib.: [4]   Rarity: rare ○

Rock Crystal
Mineralogy: clear crystal quartz (trigonal, primary)
Indications: (SP) clarity, neutrality (S) strengthens personal point of view, improves memory (M) improves perceptive faculty, increases awareness and brings clarity in thinking (B) enhances energy flow; fortifies nerves, brain, glands; alleviates pain and swellings.
Bib.: [1] [2] [3]   Rarity: common ○

Rock Crystal (Accumulation Quartz Crystal)
Mineralogy: crystal with edge-like termination (trigonal, primary)
Indications: (SP) inner composure (S) has a fortifying effect, helps concentrate energy and manage one's energy (M) promotes calm, level-headed attention (B) helps eliminate excess energy and reduce fever; clears the atmosphere in a room.
Bib.: [2]   Rarity: common ○

Rock Crystal (Channeling Quartz Crystal)
Mineralogy: quartz crystal with large seven-sided facet at apex
Indications: (SP) for receptivity (S) enhances intuition, sensitivity and mediumistic abilities, gives inner calm and makes open-minded (M) sharpens receptive faculty, aids meditation (B) improves care of one's body and its needs.
Bib.: [2]   Rarity: scarce ○

Rock Crystal (Double Termination)
Mineralogy: quartz crystal pointed at both ends (trigonal, primary)
Indications: (SP) unifies **(S)** improves contact with other beings, enhances memory and dream recall **(M)** promotes understanding, telepathy and helps express oneself clearly **(B)** improves simultaneous flow of energy in two directions and releases blockages.
Bib.: [2]   **Rarity:** not always available ○

Rock Crystal (Faden Quartz)
Mineralogy: parallel joint quartz crystal with a milky 'growth line'
Indications: (SP) healing **(S)** helps with intense inner conflict and in dealing with painful experiences **(M)** helps unify incompatibles and bridges gaps **(B)** alleviates back pain and enormously optimises self-healing power of the body.
Bib.: [4]   **Rarity:** rare ○

Rock Crystal (Generator Quartz Crystal)
Mineralogy: quartz crystal with six facets meeting equally at peak
Indications: (SP) strengthens **(S)** promotes poise, confidence, uprightness **(M)** aids in concise expression of thoughts and words **(B)** directs energy flow to the extremities and fortifies and stimulates the meridians and nerves.
Bib.: [2]   **Rarity:** not always available ○

Rock Crystal (Harmony Quartz, Self-Healed Quartz)
Mineralogy: quartz crystal with healed broken surface (trig., prim.)
Indications: (SP) amendment **(S)** helps come to terms with blows of fate and resolve conflicts in relationships **(M)** makes it possible to draw positive lessons even from painful experiences **(B)** stimulates self-healing power; helps with infections and fractures.
Bib.: [2]   **Rarity:** not always available ○

Rock Crystal (Herkimer Diamond, Herkimer Quartz)
Mineralogy: double-terminated clear quartz crystal; Herkimer, USA
Indications: (SP) awareness, clarity **(S)** improves dream recall and emotional orientation **(M)** enhances awareness and heightens consciousness **(B)** relieves pain (by placing three crystals in a triangle); supports the nerves, brain and senses.
Bib.: [2] [3]   **Rarity:** not always available ○

Rock Crystal (Laser Quartz Crystal)

Mineralogy: slender quartz crystal tapering to apex (trig., prim.)
Indications: (SP) for focussing (S) helps concentrate one's energy and mobilise reserves (M) strengthens mental intention, focuses thoughts on current goal (B) directs energy flow towards the apex; has a strong stimulating effect on the meridians and nerves.
Bib.: [2]   **Rarity:** scarce ○

Rock Crystal (Needle Quartz)

Mineralogy: slender, long prismatic quartz crystal (trigonal, primary)
Indications: (SP) energy flow, alignment (S) sets internal images, recollections and feelings into motion (M) motivates to spiritual advancement and success (B) fortifies the nerves, regulates and controls energy flow in the body, helps harmonise scars.
Bib.: [2]   **Rarity:** readily available ○

Rock Crystal (Phantom Quartz)

Mineralogy: quartz crystal w. visible marks reflecting growth stages
Indications: (SP) overcoming unhealthy boundaries (S) helps overcome fear, makes courageous (and confident in one's abilities) (M) helps overcome stagnation in thought and ability to do the 'impossible' (B) enhances growth and development of the body.
Bib.: [1] [2]   **Rarity:** readily available ○

Rock Crystal (Phantom Quartz with Chlorite)

Mineralogy: crystal with chlorite occlusion reflecting growth stages
Indications: (SP) growth, stages of development (S) gives faith and courage to face life (M) opens up unexpected new horizons and helps awaken unknown abilities (B) stimulates growth in children; aids regeneration and fortifies the immune system.
Bib.: [2]   **Rarity:** readily available ○

Rock Crystal (Receiver Quartz Crystal)

Mineralogy: quartz crystal with very large surface tip (trigonal, prim.)
Indications: (SP) brings relief (S) releases tension, has an emotionally refreshing and fortifying effect (M) helps loosen fixed attention and to better experience environment (B) has fever-reducing effect; relaxes; enhances energy flow and detoxification.
Bib.: [2] [3]   **Rarity:** readily available ○

Rock Crystal (Skeleton Quartz, Elestial)
Mineralogy: dented facets caused by rapid growth at edges
Indications: (SP) primeval knowledge (S) promotes instinctual trust,
increase in strength and swift spontaneous developments (M) helps
discover and express one's own primeval knowledge (B) enhances and
accelerates development and regeneration processes in the body.
Bib.: [2]   **Rarity:** scarce ○

Rock Crystal (Tabular Quartz Crystal)
Mineralogy: very wide flat quartz crystal (trigonal, primary)
Indications: (SP) broadens horizon (S) promotes sense of community
and putting one's own ego last (M) aids circumspection for necessities
of overriding importance, helps pass this on (B) increases physical
energy when necessary.
Bib.: [2]   **Rarity:** not always available ○

Rock Crystal (Trans-Channeling Quartz Crystal, Dow Crystal)
Mineralogy: quartz crystal with alt. three- and seven-sided facets
Indications: (SP) spiritual abilities (S) helps be in harmony with one-
self (M) helps consciously develop and train personal spiritual abilities
(B) balances energy shortages and excesses in the body organism
and promotes self-organisation.
Bib.: [2]   **Rarity:** scarce ○

Rock Crystal (Transmitter Quartz Crystal)
Mineralogy: two seven-sided facets with triangle between them
Indications: (SP) links to pure vibrations (S) helps alleviate guilty
conscience by encouraging confession, heart-to-heart talk and reconciliation (M) enhances hearing of one's inner voice (B) improves
communication with the body.
Bib.: [2]   **Rarity:** scarce ○

Rock Crystal (Window Quartz Crystal)
Mineralogy: quartz crystal w. rhombic facet below apex (trig., prim.)
Indications: (SP) self-recognition, reflection (S) brings insight into
one's emotional life, promotes untapped abilities (M) helps examine
oneself neutrally and promotes the perceptive faculty (B) helps break
resistance against recovery.
Bib.: [2]   **Rarity:** scarce ○

Rose Quartz
Mineralogy: pink-coloured quartz (silicon dioxide, trigonal, primary)
Indications: (SP) sensitivity (S) increases empathy; helps with sexual difficulties (M) clearly illuminates personal needs and the desires of others (B) harmonises heart beat and promotes strengthening of sexual organs and fertility.
Bib.: [1] [2] [3]   **Rarity:** common ○

Rose Quartz (Star Rose Quartz)
Mineralogy: rose quartz with light stars due to rutile (trigonal, prim.)
Indications: (SP) compassion (S) makes open, helpful, loving and romantic (M) enhances a harmonious living together (B) helps with diseases of the heart, blood and sexual organs, refines the senses.
Bib.: [1] [2] [3]   **Rarity:** scarce ○

Ruby
Mineralogy: corundum cont. chromium (trigonal, prim./mostly tert.)
Indications: (SP) passion, joie de vivre (S) promotes bravery, virtue and courage; sexually stimulates (M) enhances commitment and performance (B) increases fever and blood pressure; stimulates circulation, adrenal glands and sexual organs.
Bib.: [1] [2] [3]   **Rarity:** readily available ○

Ruby in Kyanite
Mineralogy: ruby in kyanite (disthene) coating (trigonal/triclinic, tert.)
Indications: (SP) determination, self-realisation (S) joie de vivre, will-power, strength (M) for managing crises/cause and effect (B) helps with nervous disease, circulation problems, irregular heartbeat and constriction of the chest.
Bib.: [4]   **Rarity:** rare ○

Ruby Kyanite Fuchsite
Mineralogy: ruby in kyanite in fuchsite (trig./tricl./ monocl., tert.)
Indications: (SP) protection and self-determination (S) composure; releases tension; relieves pain; promotes good sleep (M) aids the courage to overcome problems (B) helps with paralysis, rheumatism, inflammations, skin diseases, heart and back problems.
Bib.: –   **Rarity:** rare ○

Ruby (Star Ruby)

Mineralogy: ruby with light stars due to rutile fibre (trigonal, tertiary)
Indications: (SP) impetus, vigour and motion **(S)** promotes sensuality and sexuality; makes optimistic and cheerful **(M)** helps rightly assess one's strengths **(B)** warms, increases blood flow, stabilises circulation and fortifies the spleen and sexual organs.
Bib.: [1] [2] [3]   **Rarity:** scarce ○

Ruin Marble (Limestone)

Mineralogy: lime rock breccia (calcium carbonate, trigonal, second.)
Indications: (SP) sense of community **(S)** fortifies sense of community, faithfulness and unity **(M)** promotes team work and group consensus **(B)** stimulates calcium metabolism and fortifies the respiratory tract, large intestine, connective tissues and bones.
Bib.: [2]   **Rarity:** not always available ○

Rutilated Quartz, blue (Blue quartz group)

Mineralogy: crystal quartz with fine rutile fibre (trigonal, primary)
Indications: (SP) sense of reality **(S)** lends lightness, and a feeling of spaciousness; aids sexual control in premature ejaculation etc. **(M)** promotes pragmatic thinking and action **(B)** relieves pain, cools and reduces fever and helps with bronchitis.
Bib.: [2]   **Rarity:** not always available ○

Rutilated Quartz, clear

Mineralogy: few rutile fibres in quartz (tetragonal/trigonal, primary)
Indications: (SP) faraway feeling **(S)** frees from a feeling of suffocation and lends a feeling of being faraway and of freedom **(M)** helps develop new life concepts and face the future with optimism **(B)** helps with allergies, asthma, breathing and heart problems.
Bib.: [1] [2] [3]   **Rarity:** not always available ○

Rutilated Quartz, red

Mineralogy: red rutile fibre in quartz (tetragonal/trigonal, primary)
Indications: (SP) greatness, vision **(S)** helps with sexual problems like impotence and premature ejaculation **(M)** helps 'think big' and not to undermine one's visions **(B)** stimulates cell regeneration; helps with constipation and problems of the intestine.
Bib.: [1] [2] [3]   **Rarity:** not always available ○

Rutilated Quartz, yellow
Mineralogy: yellow rutile fibre in quartz (tetragonal/trigonal, primary)
Indications: (SP) hope, independence **(S)** lightens mood, frees from unacknowledged fear **(M)** helps liberate oneself from entanglements in situations that apparently cannot be helped **(B)** loosens up cough and helps with chronic bronchitis.
Bib.: [1] [2] [3]   **Rarity:** readily available ○

Sandrose
Mineralogy: gypsum rosette cont. sand (trigonal/monoclinic, secon.)
Indications: (SP) form and structure **(S)** stabilises experience of emotions; curbs uncontrolled outbursts **(M)** promotes a fair balance between conflicting wishes and demands **(B)** firms up connective tissues and enhances stability of the bones.
Bib.: [2]   **Rarity:** readily available ○

Sapphire
Mineralogy: corundum (aluminium oxide, trigonal, prim./mostly tert.)
Indications: (SP) spiritual power, astuteness **(S)** bestows with an unshakeable inner calm **(M)** helps collect one's thoughts and concentrate them with great strength on a goal **(B)** relieves pain, fortifies nerves and reduces fever and blood pressure.
Bib.: [1] [2]   **Rarity:** readily available ○

Sapphire (Star Sapphire)
Mineralogy: sapphire with light stars due to rutile fibres (trig., tert.)
Indications: (SP) love for truth; composure **(S)** calms and helps with depressions and hallucinations **(M)** makes sober and urges examination of the integrity and reliability of oneself and others **(B)** helps with diseases of the intestine, brain and nerves.
Bib.: [1] [2]   **Rarity:** scarce ○

Sard
Mineralogy: brown chalcedony (quartz, trigonal, primary/secondary)
Indications: (SP) inner strength **(S)** helps come to terms with disappointments; help with advice and support **(M)** helps master demanding situations **(B)** improves heart blood flow, helps with cardiac insufficiency and irregular heartbeat.
Bib.: [1] [2] [3]   **Rarity:** not always available ○

Sardonyx

Mineralogy: chalcedony/sard/onyx (trigonal, primary/secondary)

Indications: (SP) sensory perception, virtue **(S)** for honesty and strength of character **(M)** refines perception and aids its understanding **(B)** enhances all the senses, helps ear problems and tinnitus, fortifies the spleen and prevents relapses after illnesses.

Bib.: [1] [2] [3]   **Rarity:** not always available ○

Scapolite

Mineralogy: lattice silicate (tetragonal, primary/tertiary)

Indications: (SP) carefree **(S)** lightens mood; life-affirming; helps be faithful to oneself **(M)** releases obsessions; broadens thought horizons; helps breakthrough denial **(B)** helps with problems of the kidneys and eyes.

Bib.: [2]   **Rarity:** scarce ○

Selenite (Fibre Gypsum)

Mineralogy: fibrous calcium sulphate (monoclinic, secondary)

Indications: (SP) shielding, control, strong hold **(S)** calms irritation and hyperactivity; protects against loss of control; helps withdraw **(M)** for conscious perception and dissolution of personal patterns **(B)** firms up the tissues and relieves pain.

Bib.: [2]   **Rarity:** readily available ○

Septarian

Mineralogy: calcite in clay nodule (trigonal/triclinic/monocli., secon.)

Indications: (SP) makes approachable **(S)** helps remain firm in difficult situations without closing down **(M)** dissipates repressive mechanisms **(B)** helps with tumour growth, hyperacidity and intestine and skin diseases.

Bib.: [2]   **Rarity:** readily available ○

Serpentine with Chromite (Chita)

Mineralogy: serpentine with chromite (monoclinic/cubic, tertiary)

Indications: (SP) self-determination **(S)** helps shield oneself from external influences **(M)** helps better represent one's interests **(B)** helps with problems of the kidneys, liver, stomach and intestine, especially when there is an alternation of diarrhoea and constipation.

Bib.: [1] [2] [3]   **Rarity:** not always available ○

Serpentine, ('China Jade')
Mineralogy: alkaline magnesium sheet silicate (monoclinic, tertiary)
Indications: (SP) care (S) eases stress and strain; harmonises mood changes (M) promotes support and mutual help (B) helps with muscle cramps, regulates kidney function, ameliorates hyperacidity and reduces deposits in the vessels.
Bib.: [1] [2] [3]   **Rarity:** not always available ○

Serpentine (Silver Eye)
Mineralogy: serpentine with asbestos stratum (monoclinic, tertiary)
Indications: (SP) protection (S) promotes inner peace and setting bounds; helps dissolve orgasm blockages during sex (M) aids willingness to compromise and curbs quarrelsomeness (B) helps with irregular heartbeat, muscle cramps and menstrual pains.
Bib.: [1] [2] [3]   **Rarity:** readily available ○

Shiva-Lingam (Sandstone)
Mineralogy: sediment river debris (diverse structures, secondary)
Indications: (SP) spiritual advancement (S) good for coming to terms with early childhood experiences and other emotional scars (M) helps examine oneself and let go of unnecessary things (B) harmonises and decramps during abdominal discomfort.
Bib.: [2]   **Rarity:** not always available ○

Siderite
Mineralogy: iron carbonate (trigonal, all formation stages)
Indications: (SP) firmness (S) lends patience and strength in difficult times; enhances calmness in a harassed and troubled state of mind (M) helps overcome oneself and put a stop to brooding (B) good for problems of the heart, circulation and iron metabolism.
Bib.: [2]   **Rarity:** scarce ○

Snake Jasper (Fossil Foraminifera)
Mineralogy: fossilised foraminifera in clay rock (secondary)
Indications: (SP) contemplation, reflection (S) lends caution to one's involvement with others, or careful withdrawal (M) enhances the digestion of life experiences (B) stimulates the stomach, pancreas, intestine, digestion and excretion.
Bib.: [2]   **Rarity:** not always available ○

Snow Quartz (White Quartz)
Mineralogy: white coarse quartz (silicon dioxide, trigonal, primary)
Indications: (SP) support, caution **(S)** helps become aware of one's potential and to put it to use **(M)** helps express oneself neutrally and objectively **(B)** directs energy flow to undersupplied areas, helps with weakness, and strengthens the spine and joints.
Bib.: [2]   **Rarity:** readily available ○

Smithsonite
Mineralogy: zinc carbonate (trigonal, secondary)
Indications: (SP) interest **(S)** makes extravert, removes shyness; improves sleep **(M)** promotes intelligence **(B)** eases diabetes; aids wound healing, immune system and fertility; good for the skin, nerves and restless legs.
Bib.: [2]   **Rarity:** scarce ○

Sodalite
Mineralogy: lattice silicate containing sodium (cubic, primary)
Indications: (SP) search for truth **(S)** dissipates guilt; helps stand by oneself **(M)** increases consciousness, idealism and the striving for truth **(B)** enhances assimilation of fluids; helps with hoarseness, loss of voice, fever, excess weight and high blood pressure.
Bib.: [1] [2] [3]   **Rarity:** readily available ○

Sphalerite-Wurtzite (Schalenblende)
Mineralogy: sphalerite/wurtzite (zinc sulphide, cub/hexag., primary)
Indications: (SP) upheaval, transformation **(S)** helps see one through dramatic changes **(M)** ends futile brooding **(B)** good for the brain, skin, retina of the eye, sense of smell and taste, prostate and gonads; protects against harmful substances and radiations.
Bib.: [1] [2]   **Rarity:** not always available ○

Sphalerite yellow
Mineralogy: transparent zincblende (zinc sulphide, cubic, primary)
Indications: (SP) agility, vigour **(S)** good for exhaustion, weakness, despondency and fear **(M)** strengthens power of memory and helps monitor several things simultaneously **(B)** helps with diabetes and restless legs; good for the brain, skin, immune reaction and fertility.
Bib.: [2]   **Rarity:** scarce ○

Sphalerite (Zincblende)
Mineralogy: zinc sulphide (cubic, all formation stages)
Indications: (SP) swiftness **(S)** harmonises inner restlessness and helps fall asleep **(M)** promotes abstract thinking, concentration and memory **(B)** improves wound healing, eases diabetes and strengthens the brain, skin and immune reaction.
Bib.: [2]   **Rarity:** not always available ○

Sphene (Titanite)
Mineralogy: calcium titan island silicate (monoclinic, primary/tert.)
Indications: (SP) integrity **(S)** promotes self-control **(M)** helps struggle through opposition **(B)** enhances regeneration; strengthens the immune system and helps with stubborn inflammations, bronchitis, sinusitis or root canal infection of the tooth etc.
Bib.: [2]   **Rarity:** scarce ○

Spinel
Mineralogy: magnesium aluminium oxide (cubic, primary/tertiary)
Indications: (SP) self-assertion **(S)** lends courage, optimism and life-affirming attitude **(M)** promotes structure in thinking and perseverance in acting **(B)** strengthens the muscles, revives numb and paralysed limbs and cleanses the blood vessels, intestine and skin.
Bib.: [2]   **Rarity:** scarce ○

Staurolite
Mineralogy: iron aluminium island silicate (orthorhombic, tertiary)
Indications: (SP) identity, transformation of one's life **(S)** helps dissolve fixed patterns **(M)** helps differentiate between meaningful and senseless things in life **(B)** promotes a healthy environment for the body fluids; helps with bacterial, viral and fungal infections.
Bib.: [2]   **Rarity:** not always available ○

Steatite (Talc)
Mineralogy: alkaline magnesium sheet silicate (monoclinic, tertiary)
Indications: (SP) makes approachable **(S)** helps overcome fear and exaggerated defensiveness **(M)** makes easy to get along with and willing to talk **(B)** cleanses and gets rid of fatty tissue; helps with excess weight, protects the blood vessels and heart.
Bib.: [2]   **Rarity:** readily available ○

Stilbite
Mineralogy: zeolite leaves (lattice silicate, monoclinic, primary)
Indications: (SP) gentleness (S) for a calm, relaxed and confident state of mind (M) prompts to follow one's ideas and visions (B) promotes kidney function; fortifies the senses, especially the sense of taste, and helps with sore throat.
Bib.: [2]   **Rarity:** not always available ○

Stromatolite
Mineralogy: sediment formed by diatoms (secondary)
Indications: (SP) adaptability (S) allows co-operation whilst still maintaining a firm standpoint (M) helps digest experiences and mature through them (B) cleanses the intestine and tissues, improves the intestinal flora, aids metabolism and excretion.
Bib.: [2]   **Rarity:** not always available ○

Strontianite
Mineralogy: strontium carbonate (orthorhom., prim./mostly second.)
Indications: (SP) esteem (S) strengthens self-worth; lightens mood (M) enhances powers of decision-making and outgoingness (B) enhances performance and staying power; helps avoid over-exertion; improves bowel movement.
Bib.: [2]   **Rarity:** not always available ○

Sugilite
Mineralogy: ring silicate rich in mineral elements (hexagonal, prim.)
Indications: (SP) enhances awareness of consequences (S) helps remain faithful to oneself; helps with fear and paranoia (M) gives strength to resolve conflicts without compromise (B) helps with pain, nervous problems, dyslexia and disorder of the motor nerves.
Bib.: [1] [2] [3]   **Rarity:** scarce ○

Sulphur
Mineralogy: sulphur (natural element, orthorhombic, prim./second.)
Indications: (SP) purification (S) for moodiness and grubby appearance (M) reveals obscurities und hidden thoughts (B) for deep cleansing of the skin, connective tissues and adipose tissues; enhances elimination of heavy metals.
Bib.: [2]   **Rarity:** not always available ○

Sulphur Quartz
Mineralogy: sulphur-yellow crystal quartz (trigonal, primary)
Indications: (SP) purification, clarification (S) helps dissipate anger, listlessness, annoyance and fickleness (M) helps resolve conflicts sensibly and find the cause of all kinds of misery (B) promotes elimination and helps with skin impurities.
Bib.: –   Rarity: scarce ○

Sunstone (Hematite Feldspar)
Mineralogy: glittering brown feldspar (lattice silicate, triclinic, prim.)
Indications: (SP) optimism (S) life-affirming; dissipates fear, anxiety and depression (M) turns attention to personal strengths and the sunny side of life (B) harmonises the vegetative nervous system and the interplay of the organs.
Bib.: [1] [2]   Rarity: readily available ○

Tanzanite (Zoisite)
Mineralogy: blue zoisite (group silicate, orthorhombic, primary)
Indications: (SP) vocation, orientation (S) helps overcome fear and crises and build up trust (M) helps solve questions related to the meaning of life, and coming to terms with oneself (B) strengthens nerves and kidneys, and has a fortifying and supporting effect.
Bib.: [2]   Rarity: rare ○

Tektite
Mineralogy: glass formed by meteorite impact (amorphous)
Indications: (SP) letting go (S) helps let go of fear of the future and obsession with money or possessions (M) aids recognition that one is a spiritual being (B) accelerates healing; helps with damages caused both by radiations and by infectious diseases.
Bib.: [2]   Rarity: readily available ○

Thulite (Zoisite)
Mineralogy: manganese zoisite (group silicate, orthorhombic, tert.)
Indications: (SP) pleasure, challenge (S) helps overcome one's limitations; stimulates romance and sexuality (M) helps live out desires, imaginations and needs (B) enhances fertility and regeneration; strengthens the sexual organs.
Bib.: [1] [2] [3]   Rarity: not always available ○

Tiger's Eye
Mineralogy: yellowish brown fibrous quartz (trigonal, secondary)
Indications: (SP) gives overview; reserve (S) helps with stress, strain and assailing external currents (M) sharpens the senses and helps maintain overview when things are happening fast (B) regulates the adrenal glands; relieves asthma attacks.
Bib.: [1] [2] [3]   Rarity: common ○

Tiger's Eye with Falcon's Eye (Multicoloured Tiger's Eye)
Mineralogy: falcon's eye transforming into tiger's eye (trig., second.)
Indications: (SP) enhances composure, reserve (S) helps remain composed in extreme situations (M) enhances quick intellectual grasp and well-thought-out actions (B) relieves pain; regulates the adrenal glands; helps with acute asthma attacks.
Bib.: [1] [2]   Rarity: readily available ○

Tiger Iron
Mineralogy: hematite, jasper and tiger's eye rock (trigonal, tertiary)
Indications: (SP) life energy (S) helps overcome difficulties (M) helps carry out pragmatic solutions rapidly with determination (B) helps with exhaustion, circulation problems, lack of iron and promotes blood formation and oxygen transportation.
Bib.: [1] [2] [3]   Rarity: readily available ○

Topaz, blue
Mineralogy: aluminium island silicate cont. iron (orthorho., primary)
Indications: (SP) self-confidence (S) makes reliable and secure in one's abilities (M) helps gain wisdom from the twists of fate (B) strengthens the nerves, improves digestion and assimilation of nutrients.
Bib.: [1] [2] [3]   Rarity: scarce ○

Topaz Imperial (Golden Topaz)
Mineralogy: aluminium silicate cont. phosphorus (orthorh., prim.)
Indications: (SP) self-confidence (S) helps present oneself in favourable light; helps with depression (M) helps realise great plans (B) helps with nerve problems, digestion and eating disorders (including anorexia); enhances metabolism and fertility in women.
Bib.: [1] [2] [3]   Rarity: scarce ○

Topaz, white (Silver Topaz)
Mineralogy: aluminium island silicate (orthorhombic, primary)
Indications: (SP) self-realisation (S) helps discover one's inner wealth of knowledge and abilities (M) enhances spiritual development; helps clearly recognise one's objectives (B) helps with bad eyesight and eye problems; stimulates metabolism.
Bib.: [1] [2] [3]　　　　　　　　**Rarity:** readily available ◯

Topaz, yellow
Mineralogy: aluminium island silicate cont. chrome (orthorh., prim.)
Indications: (SP) self-worth (S) promotes self-assurance and consciousness of one's importance (M) helps acknowledge achievements and one's actions in life (B) stimulates digestion and metabolism; strengthens the stomach, pancreas and small intestine.
Bib.: [1] [2] [3]　　　　　　　　　　　**Rarity:** scarce ◯

Tourmaline, black (Schorl)
Mineralogy: black iron aluminium tourmaline (trigonal, primary)
Indications: (SP) neutrality (S) promotes relaxation, eases stress, protects from external influences, improves sleep (M) makes objective, clear, logical and rational (B) helps with effects of radiations, pain, strain, feeling of numbness, and screens scars.
Bib.: [1] [2] [3]　　　　　　　　**Rarity:** readily available ◯

Tourmaline, blue (Indigolite)
Mineralogy: blue tourmaline (boron ring silicate, trigonal, primary)
Indications: (SP) faithfulness and ethics (S) dissipates grief and blocked emotions (M) makes open and tolerant; enhances love for truth and sense of responsibility (B) stimulates water balance and excretion through kidneys and bladder; helps heal burns.
Bib.: [1] [2] [3]　　　　　　　　　　　**Rarity:** scarce ◯

Tourmaline Cat's Eye
Mineralogy: fibrous tourmaline with glimmer of light (trigonal, prim.)
Indications: (SP) imagination (S) stimulates the drawing on a rich inner world of images (M) brings new perspectives, shows the beauty in everything (B) for nerves, perceptory senses, detoxification, excretion and joints; effective for the head and respiratory tract.
Bib.: [2]　　　　　　　　　　　　　　**Rarity:** scarce ◯

Tourmaline (Dravite)
Mineralogy: magnesium aluminium tourmaline (trigonal, primary)
Indications: (SP) sense of community (S) promotes willingness to help, and social commitment (M) endows with pragmatic creativity and craft skills (B) stimulates regeneration of the cells, tissues and skin; helps with cellulite and healing of scars.
Bib.: [1] [2] [3]　　　　　　　　**Rarity:** not always available ○

Tourmaline, green (Verdelite)
Mineralogy: green tourmaline (boron ring silicate, trigonal, primary)
Indications: (SP) gratitude (S) helps see the miracles of life (M) promotes interest in fellow human beings and the environment (B) detoxifies, strengthens the nerves, heart, intestine, joints and functional tissue (parenchyma); helps with degenerative processes and tumours.
Bib.: [1] [2] [3]　　　　　　　　**Rarity:** not always available ○

Tourmaline (Paraiba Tourmaline)
Mineralogy: tourmaline cont. copper (boron ring silicate, trig., prim.)
Indications: (SP) love, beauty (S) helps experience an all-embracing love for the world and all beings; gives intense dreams (M) promotes justice, decision-making; clears confusion (B) stimulates the hormones, liver, nerves and brain.
Bib.: [2]　　　　　　　　　　　**Rarity:** rare ○

Tourmaline polychrome (Elbaite)
Mineralogy: multicoloured tourmaline (boron ring silicate, trig. prim.)
Indications: (SP) wholeness: brings spirit, soul, mind and body into a harmonious wholeness (S) enhances imagination and dreams (M) helps recognise and control developments (B) harmonises the nerves, metabolism, hormonal glands and immune system.
Bib.: [1] [2] [3]　　　　　　　　**Rarity:** scarce ○

Tourmaline, red (Rubellite)
Mineralogy: red tourmaline (boron ring silicate, trigonal, primary)
Indications: (SP) liveliness (S) makes sociable, lively and lends joy in sexuality (M) helps dedicated commitment (B) strengthens the function of the nerves, blood, spleen, liver, heart and sexual organs.
Bib.: [1] [2] [3]　　　　　　　　**Rarity:** not always available ○

Tourmaline, violet (Apyrite)
Mineralogy: violet tourmaline (boron ring silicate, trigonal, primary)
Indications: (SP) wisdom **(S)** promotes deep peace of mind and helps see life from an optimistic viewpoint **(M)** helps find the right solutions to problems **(B)** harmonises the nervous system and hormonal balance; regulates breathing, the brain and intestines.
Bib.: [2]   **Rarity:** scarce ○

Tourmaline (Watermelon Tourmaline)
Mineralogy: green tourmaline with a red core (trigonal, primary)
Indications: (SP) understanding **(S)** promotes love, friendship and security; dispels fear and depression **(M)** helps express one's intentions clearly **(B)** strengthens the heart, promotes regeneration of the nerves, helps with paralysis and multiple sclerosis.
Bib.: [1] [2] [3]   **Rarity:** scarce ○

Tourmaline, yellow
Mineralogy: yellow tourmaline (boron ring silicate, trigonal, primary)
Indications: (SP) happiness **(S)** bestows contentment to a life, and confidence in one's abilities **(M)** enhances memory, desire to undertake things and a positive world view **(B)** stimulates the senses, nerves, digestion and metabolism.
Bib.: [1] [2]   **Rarity:** scarce ○

Tourmaline Quartz
Mineralogy: tourmaline needles (schorl) in quartz (trigonal, primary)
Indications: (SP) links polarities **(S)** helps resolve inner battles and conflicts **(M)** helps bring contrasts into harmony **(B)** releases tension, uptightness and hardening; keeps vital and mobile, promotes purification and excretion; fortifies the nerves.
Bib.: [1] [2] [3]   **Rarity:** readily available ○

Tree Agate (Quartz)
Mineralogy: white quartz with green inclusions (trigonal, primary)
Indications: (SP) inner peace, incontestability **(S)** security, stability and perseverance even in unpleasant situations **(M)** helps accept and master challenges **(B)** makes more resistant and enhances immune system, helps in cases of high susceptibility to infections.
Bib.: [1] [2]   **Rarity:** readily available ○

Tugtupite

Mineralogy: sheet silicate cont. sodium (tetragonal, primary)

Indications: **(SP)** conviction, understanding **(S)** enhances self-confidence; dissipates feelings of revenge and self-pity **(M)** ends self-doubt and regret; helps learn from mistakes and stand up for one's convictions **(B)** helps with heart and kidney problems.

Bib.: [2] **Rarity:** rare ○

Turquoise

Mineralogy: alkaline copper aluminium phosphate (triclinic, second.)

Indications: **(SP)** fate **(S)** harmonises, cheers and protects from external influences **(M)** helps recognise causes of happiness and unhappiness and master them **(B)** helps with exhaustion, hyperacidity, rheumatism, gout, stomach pains and cramps.

Bib.: [1] [2] [3] **Rarity:** not always available ○

Ulexite

Mineralogy: sodium calcium hydrogen borate (triclinic, secondary)

Indications: **(SP)** attention **(S)** has a restorative and stabilising effect in cases of sudden depressions and feelings of faintness **(M)** helps attentive observation for how things really are **(B)** strengthens the nerves, helps with nausea and eye problems.

Bib.: [2] **Rarity:** rare ○

Vanadinite

Mineralogy: lead vanadate (hexagonal, secondary)

Indications: **(SP)** self-conquest **(S)** helps overcome feelings of desolation, destruction and helplessness **(M)** helps overcome paralysing issues **(B)** addresses latent illnesses; helps with stubborn inflammations.

Bib.: [2] **Rarity:** scarce ○

Variscite

Mineralogy: hydrous aluminium phosphate (orthorhomb., second.)

Indications: **(SP)** cheers up **(S)** helps with chronic tiredness; eases inner restlessness **(M)** makes objective and rational; helps express oneself clearly **(B)** gives energy, alleviates hyperacidity, helps with heartburn, gastritis, stomach ulcers, rheumatism and gout.

Bib.: [1] [2] [3] **Rarity:** not always available ○

Verdite (Fuchsite Serpentine Clay)
Mineralogy: fuchsite w. serpentine &/or clay mineral (monocl., sec.)
Indications: (SP) alertness **(S)** helps perceive external influences; makes stable and able to cope with stress **(M)** helps take responsibility for one's actions **(B)** aids deacidification, cleansing and elimination; strengthens the stomach, liver and intestine.
Bib.: [1] [2]   **Rarity:** not always available ○

Vesuvianite (Californite)
Mineralogy: rock containing vesuvian (vesuvian: tetragonal, tert.)
Indications: (SP) honesty, interest and enquiring mind **(S)** helps change strong vices and behavioural patterns **(M)** incites heart-to-heart talk to clear annoyance and disappointment **(B)** promotes deacidification and regeneration; anti-inflammatory.
Bib.: [2]   **Rarity:** not always available ○

Vesuvianite (Idocrase)
Mineralogy: group silicate rich in mineral elements (tetragonal, tert.)
Indications: (SP) honesty; enquiring mind; helps overcome habits and fear **(M)** helps consciously do away with masks and façades **(B)** promotes regeneration; strengthens the liver and nerves; de-acidifies; anti-inflammatory.
Bib.: [2]   **Rarity:** scarce ○

Vivianite
Mineralogy: hydrous iron phosphate (monoclinic, secondary)
Indications: (SP) intensity **(S)** livens up, frees from buried emotion, makes life intensive and exciting **(M)** helps with boredom and shakes up rusty relationships **(B)** de-acidifies; stimulates the liver; helps with weakness and lack of energy.
Bib.: [2]   **Rarity:** rare ○

Wardite
Mineralogy: sodium aluminium phosphate (tetragonal, secondary)
Indications: (SP) honesty, frankness **(S)** helps show oneself how one is **(M)** makes it easier to resolve relationship conflicts **(B)** has a restorative and strengthening effect; helps with hyperacidity and problems of the kidneys, urinary tract and bladder.
Bib.: [4]   **Rarity:** rare ○

Wollastonite
Mineralogy: calcium chain silicate (triclinic, tertiary)
Indications: (SP) stability and foothold (S) aids resistance against emotional attacks (M) great determination; consolidates personal convictions (B) promotes the tissues, growth, awareness of the body, posture and coordination of body movements.
Bib.: [2]   **Rarity:** scarce ○

Wulfenite (Yellow Lead Ore)
Mineralogy: lead molybdate (tetragonal, secondary)
Indications: (SP) freedom of movement (S) frees from compulsive restraints (M) helps recognise tensions and patterns determined in upbringing and handle them more freely (B) helps with calluses, dryness, emaciation, muscular atrophy and lithogenesis.
Bib.: [2]   **Rarity:** scarce ○

Zircon
Mineralogy: zirconium island silicate (tetragonal, primary)
Indications: (SP) purpose of existence (S) helps overcome losses and let go of possessiveness (M) endows with recognition of what belongs to the past and what is really important (B) stimulates the liver, relieves pain, releases cramps, helps with delayed menstruation.
Bib.: [1] [2] [3]   **Rarity:** not always available ○

Zoisite
Mineralogy: calcium aluminium group silicate (orthorhombic, tert.)
Indications: (SP) regeneration, constructiveness (S) enhances regeneration after illnesses or heavy strains (M) helps detach oneself from adaptation to/and external control (B) anti-inflammatory effect; strengthens the regeneration of the cells and tissues.
Bib.: [1] [2] [3]   **Rarity:** readily available ○

Zoisite with Ruby (Anyolite)
Mineralogy: ruby in zoisite matrix (trigonal/orthorhombic, tertiary)
Indications: (SP) dynamic, regeneration (S) revives buried feelings, enhances potency (M) promotes creative commitment (B) deacidifies, regenerates and enhances fertility; good for problems of the spleen, prostate, testicles and ovaries.
Bib.: [1] [2] [3]   **Rarity:** not always available ○

Search Register

Alumstone: Alunite

Amegreen: Prasiolite Amethyst

Amulet stone: Agate (Star Agate)

Andean Opal: Opal (Andean Opal colourless, Chrysopal, Pink Opal)

Angelite: Anhydrite

Anyolite: Zoisite with Ruby

Apache Tear: Obsidian (Smoky Obs.)

Apricot-Agate: Agate, pink

Apyrite: Tourmaline, violet

Aqualite: Cat's Eye Quartz

Bixbite: Beryl, red

Black Opal: Opal (Precious O., black)

Blackstone: Gabbro

Blood Agate: Agate, red

Blood Chalcedony: Chalcedony, red

Bloodstone: Heliotrope

Blue Quartz: Aventurine blue, Rutilated Quartz blue

Boji's: Pop-Rocks

Boulder Opal: Opal (Precious Opal)

Brecciated Jasper: Jasper (Brecciated Jasper)

Buddstone: Prase Quartz

Cacoxenite: Goethite quartz

Calcentine: Ammolite

Californite: Vesuvianite

Cappuccino Jasper: Jasper, beige-brown

Carnelian yellow: Chalcedony, yellow

Cat's Eye: Chrysoberyl

Chevron-Amethyst: Amethyst (banded)

Chrome Chalcedony: Chalcedony

Chrysanthemenstone: Porphyrite

Chrysolite: Peridote

Chrysopal: Opal (Chrysopal)

Chita: Serpentine with Chromite

Cinnabarite: Cinnabar

Citron Chrysoprase: Lemon Chrysoprase

Connemara: Ophicalcite

Copper Chalcedony: Chalcedony

Coral: Agatised Coral

Crystal Opal: Opal (Precious Opal)

Cyanite: Disthene

Dalmatian Stone: Aplite Dendritic Opal: Opal (Dendritic Opal)

Dendritic Agate: Agate (Dendritic Agate)

Dendritic Chalcedony: Chalcedony

Dichroite: Cordierite

Dr. Liesegang Stone: Rhyolite

Dravite: Tourmaline (Dravite)

Dunite: Olivine, Spanish

Precious Opal: Opal (Precious Opal)

Elestial: Rock Crystal (Skeleton Quartz)

Emerald Quartz: Emerald in Matrix

Enhydro: Agate (Water Agate)

Eye Agate: Agate (Eye Agate), Ocean Jasper

Eye Jasper: Rhyolite

Faden Quartz: Rock Crystal (Faden Quartz)

Feldspar: Albite, Amazonite, Feldspar (Multicoloured Feldspar), Labradorite, Moonstone, Orthoclase, Sunstone

Fire Agate: Agate (Fire Agate)

Firestone: Flint

Flint coloured: Hornstone, coloured

Flower Porphyry: Porphyrite

Foggy Quartz: Girasol (Foggy Quartz)

Fossilised Wood: Petrified Wood

Gagate: Jet

Gem Silica: Chrysocolla-Chalcedony

Gold sheen Obsidian: Obsidian

Golden Topaz: Topaz Imperial

Goldorthoclase: Orthoclase

Goshenite: Beryl, colourless

Green Quartz: Aventurine green, Prase Quartz, Prasiolite Amethyst

Grossular: Garnet Grossular

Gypsum: Alabaster, Selenite

Heavy Spar: Barite

Herkimer: Rock Crystal (Herkimer)

Hessonite: Garnet (Hessonite)

Honey Calcite: Calcite, honey-coloured

Hyalite: Opal (Hyalite)

Idocrase: Vesuvianite (Idocrase)

Indigolite: Tourmaline, blue

Iolite Sunstone: Cordierite

Iolite: Cordierite

Iron Oolite: Oolite

Iron Ore: Hematite banded

Iron-Jasper: Jasper with Hematite

Ivorite: Dolomite (Ivorite)

Ivory Jasper: Jasper beige

Jade: Jadeite, Nephrite

Kalahari Picture Stone: Jasper (Landscape Jasper)

Korite: Ammolite

Kyanite: Disthene

Lace-Agate: Agate (Lace-Agate)

Landscape Jasper: Jasper

Lemon Calcite: Calcite, yellow

Leopard Opal: Opal in Matrix

Leopard Skin Jasper: Rhyolite

Limestone: Picasso Marble, Ruin Marble

Mahogany Obsidian: Obsidian

Mangano Calcite: Calcite, pink

Margarita: Lime Oolite

Meteorite: Iron Nickel Meteorite

Milk Opal: Opal, white

Morion: Smoky Quartz, dark

Moss Opal: Opal (Moss Opal)

Mother-of-pearl: Abalone Paua shell

Multicoloured Feldspar: Feldspar (Multicoloured Feldspar)

Natural Glass: Glass (Natural)

Nebula stone: Eldarite

Nickel Pyrite: Nickeline

Olivine: Peridote

Opal Wood: Petrified Wood (opalised)

Orange Calcite: Calcite, orange

Orbicular Jasper: Ocean Jasper

Palm Wood: Petrified Wood

Paraiba Tourmaline: Tourmaline

Paua shell: Abalone Paua shell

Peace Agate: Agate, white

Peanut Wood: Petrified Wood

Pectolite: Larimar

Peridotite: Olivine, Spanish

Petoskey Stone: Agatised Coral

Phantom Quartz: Rock Crystal (Phantom Quartz), Smoky Quartz with Phantom

Picture Jasper: Jasper, brownish-grey

Pink Opal: Opal (Pink Opal)

Poppy Jasper: Jasper (Poppy Jasper)

Prase Opal: Opal (Prase Opal)

Pyrite Balls: Pop-Rocks

Rainbow fluorite: fluorite multi-coloured
Rainbow Moonstone: Labradorite white
Rainbow Obsidian: Obsidian
Rainforest Jasper: Rhyolite
Rainforest Rhyolite: Rhyolite
Raspberry Quartz: Aventurine red
Roe Stone: Lime Oolite
Rose Chalcedony: Chalcedony pink
Rubellite: Tourmaline red
Ruby Zoisite: Zoisite with Ruby
Salt Crystal: Halite
Salt Stone: Halite
Salt: Halite
Sambesite: Prasiolite Amethyst
Sandstone: Printstone, Shiva-Lingam
Schorl: Tourmaline, black
Shell: Abalone Paua shell

Silver Eye: Serpentine (Silver Eye)
Silver Sheen Obsidian: Obsidian
Skeleton Quartz: Rock Crystal (Skeleton Quartz)
Smoky Obsidian: Obsidian
Snowflake Epidote: Epidote Feldspar
Snowflake Obsidian: Obsidian
Spectrolite: Labradorite (Spectro-lite)
Spodumene: Hiddenite, Kunzite
Star Agate: Agate (Star Agate)
Star diopside: Diopside (Star diopside)
Star Rose Quartz: Rose Quartz (Star Rose Quartz)
Star Ruby: Ruby (Star Ruby)
Star Sapphire: Sapphire (Star Sapphire)
Sugar Dolomite: Dolomite, white
Syenite: Larvikite

Talc: Steatite
Thunderegg: Agate (Star Agate)
Tiger's Eye blue = Falcon's Eye
Tiger's Eye Quartz: Gold Quartz
Titanite: Sphene
Turitella Agate: Jasper (Turitella Jasper)
Unakite: Epidote Feldspar (Unakite)
Vanadium Beryl: Beryl
Verd Antique: Ophicalcite
Verdelite: Tourmaline, green
Vulcan Jasper: Jasper (Vulcan Jasper)
Water Agate: Agate (Water Agate)
Water Opal: Opal (Hyalite)
Watermelon Tourmaline: Tour-maline
Yowah Opal: Opal (Precious Opal)
Zebra Agate: Agate, white/black
Zebra Marble: Marble, black/white
Zincblende: Sphalerite

Contact

You can reach me through Michael Gienger GmbH with questions, criticism, suggestions and additional information. Information on seminars and training courses in the field of gem therapy can also be obtained from here.

Michael Gienger GmbH, Stäudach 58/1, D-72074 Tübingen
Tel./Fax: +49 (0)70 71 - 364 720, buecher@michael-gienger.de
www.michael-gienger.de, www.steinheilkunde.de

Bibliography

[1] Michael Gienger, *Crystal Power, Crystal Healing*, Cassell, London 1998
[2] Michael Gienger, *Lexikon der Heilsteine*, Neue Erde, Saarbrücken 2000
[3] Michael Gienger, *Die Heilsteine Hausapotheke*, Neue Erde, Saarbrücken 1999
[4] Melody, *Love is in the Earth*, Earth-Love Publishing House, Wheat Ridge, Colorado 1995

(The preceding numbers refer to literature indicated under the individual gem-stone descriptions in this guide.)

Thanks

My heartfelt thanks go first and foremost to Ute Weigel in Wuppertal, whose request for a wider scope to my book, *Crystal Power, Crystal Healing* set the ball rolling. Thus my work on the gemstone guide, begun originally in 1993, came to completion 10 years later. Above all, my special thanks go to Annette Jakobi from Cairn Elen for her untiring research efforts, Walter von Holst for all information, comments and corrections related to gem remedies, Bernhard Bruder from EPI for the gemstone analysis and correction of the mineralogical specifications, Ines Blersch in Stuttgart for the hard task of photographing 430 gemstones from their respective best positions and Fred Hageneder from Dragon Design for the superb feat of transforming this thick bundle of information into a compact pocketbook. Of course, I also wish to heartily thank Andreas Lentz, my publisher, for patiently putting up with the continuously postponed deadlines. And I'm very grateful for the effort Arwen Lentz, Chinwendu Uzodike and Roselle Angwin have put into the correct translation of the English edition!

In addition, my thanks to all those who made this Gemstone Guide possible through their contributions and information on current gemstones, healing effects and availability, as well as all those who allowed me dig into their collections in search of suitable 'photographic models': Franca Bauer, Ruth and Werner Berger, Wolfgang Dei, Beate Diederich, Erwin Engelhardt, Erik Fey, Dagmar Fleck, Manfred Flinzner, Margarete Gebbers, Joachim Goebel, Claire Herrmann, Walter von Holst, Annette and Dieter Jakobi, Ava Keller, Tim Lemke, Peter Lind, Ursula and Joachim Neumann, Peter Peiner, Sabine Schneider-Kühnle, Marco Schreier, Anita Schöpf, Karl-Heinz Schwarz, Andreas Stucki, Kerstin Wagner and Sarala Zimper.

Cairn Elen

After Elen had accomplished her wandering through the world, she placed a Cairn at the end of the Sarn Elen. Her path then led her back to the land between evening and morning. From this Cairn originated all stones that direct the way at crossroads up until today.[1]

(From a Celtic myth)

'Cairn Elen'* is the term used in Gaelic-speaking areas to refer to the ancient slab stones on track ways. They mark the spiritual paths, both the paths of the earth and that of knowledge.

These paths are increasingly falling into oblivion. Just as the old paths of the earth disappear under the modern asphalt streets, so also does certain ancient wisdom disappear under the data flood of modern information. For this reason, the desire and aim of the Edition Cairn Elen is to preserve ancient wisdom and link it with modern knowledge – for a flourishing future!

The Edition Cairn Elen in Neue Erde Verlag is published by Michael Gienger. The objective of the Edition is to present knowledge from research and tradition that has remained unpublished up until now. Areas of focus are nature, naturopathy and health as well as consciousness and spiritual freedom.

Apart from current specialised literature, stories, fairytales, novels, lyric and artistic publications will also be published within the scope of Edition Cairn Elen. The knowledge thus transmitted reaches out not only to the intellect but also to the heart.

Contact

Edition Cairn Elen, Michael Gienger, Stäudach 58/1, D-72074 Tübingen
Tel: +49 (0)7071 - 364719, Fax: +49 (0)7071 - 38868,
eMail: buecher@michael-gienger.de, Website: www.michael-gienger.de

---

[1]Celtic 'cairn' [pronounced: carn] = 'Stone' (usually placed as an intentional shaped heap of stones), 'sarn' = 'Path', 'Elen, Helen' = 'Goddess of the Roads'
*Cairn Elen: in British ancient and contemporary Celtic culture, cairns are generally intentionally heaped piles of stones, rather than an individual stone such as a boulder or standing stone.

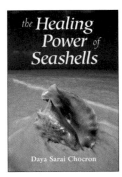

The Healing Power of Seashells
Daya Sarai Chocron

A quick guide to Seashells and their healing powers for everyone. This ancient Hawaiian wisdom is simple to understand and easy to put into practice. Included for your easy reference are photographs of Seashells and relevant descriptions to help you identify them. Most of the Seashells featured can be found on shores all over the world, and many are available for sale. This colourful book will immediately transport you to the beach!

For further information and book catalogue contact:
Findhorn Press, 305a The Park, Forres IV36 3TE, Scotland.
Earthdancer Books is an Imprint of Findhorn Press.

tel +44 (0)1309-690 582   fax +44 (0)1309-690 036
info@findhornpress.com
www.earthdancer.co.uk   www.findhornpress.com

EARTHDANCER

A FINDHORN PRESS IMPRINT